WHY BELIEVE IN ADAM?

by

Graham A. Fisher, M.Ed.

EYE-OPENER PUBLICATIONS

Open my eyes that I may behold wonderful things out of Your law. Ps 119:18

By the same author:
Speak Through the Earthquake, Wind and Fire.
Countyvise, 1/3 Grove Road, Rock Ferry, Birkenhead, Merseyside L42 3XS. 1982.

The Bible text is from the Revised Standard Version Bible, copyright 1946, 1952, 1971 by the Division of Christian Education of the National Council of the Churches of Christ in the USA, and is used by permission.

First published 1990 by EYE-OPENER PUBLICATIONS
36 Hallville Road, Mossley Hill, Liverpool, L18 0HR.
Copyright © Graham A. Fisher 1990
Photoset and printed by Birkenhead Press, 1/3 Grove Road, Rock Ferry, Birkenhead, Merseyside L42 3XS
ISBN 0 9514359 0 6. Why Believe in Adam?

All rights reserved. No part of this publication may be reproduced, stored in a retrieval system, or transmitted, in any form, or by any means, electronic, chemical, mechanical, photocopying, recording or otherwise, without the prior permission of the publisher.

ACKNOWLEDGEMENTS

My grateful thanks are extended to all of the members of the Liverpool church of Christ who not only encouraged me but who also funded publication. My special thanks go to Adrian Hill for his positive help and to Peter Anti for his enthusiastic support.

My thanks too are extended to all of my Christian brothers and sisters nationally who showed positive interest in the book and who provided us in Liverpool with the stimulus needed to proceed in faith believing that this publishing venture will not be a financial albatross around our necks.

Graham A. Fisher
January 1990

To my wife, Barbara

CONTENTS

		Page
Preface		7
Introduction		9
Chapter 1	Faith's Rationality	13
Chapter 2	In The Beginning God	21
Chapter 3	God Created	29
Chapter 4	Biting Miseries	40
Chapter 5	A World Without Adam	52
Chapter 6	If Adam Had Not Sinned	57
Chapter 7	The Rôle of The Sexes	62
Chapter 8	Judgement and Hell	74
Chapter 9	Faith and Works	82
Chapter 10	Adam and Jesus	87
Bibliography		95

PREFACE

As I grow older in the Christian faith, I find that some things get easier to understand. It is not that I have reached great theological heights or am a spiritual titan but rather that I have resolved the question of Adam in my mind and find that within the first eleven chapters of Genesis lies the key to the Scriptures and to the physical world at large.

The physical world is not my concern in this book, although inevitably it will filter into the text, but I find that my theological life is far easier with Adam than without him. To many this may appear to be a regression into spiritual naïvety or a reluctance to face up to the theological consequences of current scientific thought. However the simple truth is that those who do not accept a literal Adam, i.e. Theistic Evolutionists, have tremendous spiritual and theological difficulties, if they really think these matters through.

To believe in Adam, on the other hand, presents me with the problem of interpreting the physical world within the theological framework of a belief in special Creation. My first book, *Speak Through the Earthquake, Wind and Fire,* addresses itself to that problem in part and shows how the Bible can be interpreted more easily against an astro-catastrophic backcloth to the physical world. In this volume I want to look at some issues in religion which are directly affected by a belief in Adam and to show why I find it spiritually and theologically far more satisfactory, no matter what other problems it creates, to say, *"I believe in Adam",* and therefore to pose the question, *"Why believe in Adam?"*

Graham A. Fisher

INTRODUCTION

To say, "I believe in Adam" is not the same as saying, "I believe in Julius Caesar." Julius Caesar was no doubt a very interesting man whose life merits useful study, however, studying Julius Caesar carries no theological, philosophical, or scientific undertones. Saying, "I believe in Julius Caesar," in the sense that, "I believe there was a man of that name who lived as the histories declare," does not do violation to my world view, or to my intellectual preferences. Julius Caesar's existence as presented to me in the texts, whether correctly related or not, leaves me dispassionately neutral. This cannot be so with Adam.

The reality of the existence of Adam can never be merely an intellectual exercise since the outcome of my conclusion is not of the 'take-it-or-leave-it' variety. To conclude about Adam definitely carries tremendous implications for my life.

Adam, of course, is the central figure in the Creation v. Evolution debate and I believe this debate is the modern version of the debate over the existence or not of God. It has to be admitted that there are plenty of theists who believe firmly in God but who most definitely reject a belief in Adam as a literal, historical figure on a par with Julius Caesar. They would not see this as an 'existence of God' issue at all. They are mistaken. Not only that, they are being both theologically and scientifically inconsistent, if they sit down and think about it.

It is not just a case of demonstrating the inconsistencies in Evolution which should concern Creationists; they should be able to demonstrate rationally and fully the consistencies of their own beliefs. There are many books being written at the academic level which address themselves to the presentation of a credible view of Creation on a scientific basis, (see the Bibliography). This book however delves into some of the theological implications behind a belief in Adam and maintains that consistent Christian theology cannot be sustained without such a belief. It extends beyond Adam to the end of Genesis 11 since the events up to and immediately beyond the Flood are an integral part of the argument. A belief in a literal Adam presupposes an acceptance of a literal, global Flood and a real Ark with a real Noah and real animals in it.

ADAM — THE MAN

Biblically Adam is a very important figure yet he flits somewhat enigmatically across its pages. He is blamed for introducing sin into the world yet it was Eve who first sinned. The reason seems to be that, whereas Eve was deceived, Adam was not. She was tricked into sinning but Adam, for reasons not revealed in Scripture, sinned deliberately, knowing full well what he was doing (1 Tim. 2:14). It is his guilt which is the major concern of the Scriptures and not his biography. So what can we glean about Adam the Man?

Apart from the biographical detail in Genesis 2 and 3, which concentrates on a very small part of his life, we learn very little.

The end of Genesis 4 details the birth of Seth, as a replacement son for Abel, and the opening of Genesis 5 tells us that he had 'other sons and daughters' (v.4). We know too that he died at the ripe old age of 930 (Gen. 5:5). This may not seem to be much to go on but there is an implicit biography behind these scant details.

It is a popular question in biblical quizzes to ask, "Who was the oldest man who ever lived and how old was he?". Back would come the answer from the biblically erudite, "Methuselah — 969 years." Technically this is correct but the question could be asked, "How old was Adam when he was created?". To ask such a question is to begin to probe an important point in the Creation/Evolution debate. If God did indeed create the world in six days, He had to create an appearance of age or provide physical conditions which would produce an apparently old Earth in a short time. Barry Setterfield addresses the latter problem in his monograph, *The Velocity Of Light and The Age Of The Universe,* where he postulates that the speed of light has not been constant and that at the time of Creation it was falling rapidly from infinity to something like (though still much faster than) ours today. Be that as it may, on day 6 when Adam was created he was created as a full-grown man. Had we met him an hour after God made him he would have appeared to be twenty, thirty or even forty. Given the longer life-spans of those days we would need to add Adam's apparent age to his real age to arrive at his actual age at death. He could have easily died as an 'older' man than Methuselah!

From the moment God made him, Adam could talk, think maturely, appreciate aesthetic matters and know how to survive. His speech did not evolve (he named the animals Gen. 2:19-20), nor was it primitive. Not for him the learning of life's lessons at his mother's knee. He never knew the blessing of receiving parental love, nor the traumas of puberty, puppy love, learning to shave or finding a job!

He did not have to learn to cook, plough or sow since he was complete in every way one minute after God made him. Eve too did not go through menarche or the female equivalent of growing up. She was fully adult, capable of having children, being equipped physically and mentally for it, and ready to bear her firstborn nine months later; though we do not know how long after Creation that Cain was born.

Artists, I believe, in the Middle Ages, used to agonize over whether to paint Adam and Eve with navels or not. Since neither had a physical mother, they never needed nor had an umbilical cord. The artists aimed for theological consistency in their art, and that is to their credit, but aiming at theological consistency at all levels is vitally necessary and a part of any reason for a belief in Adam.

After the Fall, Adam had to toil and sweat to earn his living and Eve bore many children, male and female (Gen. 5:4). It is no problem to decide where Cain got his wife; she was one of his sisters. But it is a problem to decide if Adam and Eve are to be considered as of the saved or lost. It may however be possible to form an opinion.

The names 'Adam' and 'Eve' are quite popular for children within Christendom as a whole. Thus there is the tacit acceptance of their salvation by believers down the years. This, of course, is no guarantee of acceptance by God since men are notoriously easily deceived in this area but it certainly appears that a good case can be presented on their behalf. They obviously taught their children to follow God. The story of Cain and Abel implies this. There is no need to doubt that the lads got their desire to sacrifice to God, and their instructions about what to do, from their parents. The naming of the boys (Gen. 4:1, 25) and the time of calling on the name of the Lord (Gen. 4:26) would indicate that God was given a central place in their home.

They knew the joy of faithful children and the sorrow of rebels. They learnt the pain of mourning and hurt of seeing Cain, their beloved firstborn, rejected by God. They were alive to witness the great godlessness of Cain's offspring (see Gen. 4:23) but Adam at least witnessed the great godliness of Enoch who was so righteous before God that he did not taste death. He knew all the great antediluvian patriarchs except Noah so he (they) were actively working for God down to the ninth generation. They experienced success and failure in their children like most parents. Their lives would have been full of the same joys and sorrows we all feel but their sorrows would be more intense as they realized that the great wickedness and evil they saw in the world was down to their disobedience. Nevertheless Adam is listed in the genealogy of the faithful in Luke 3 and it seems reasonable to conclude that Christendom has got it right — they are amongst the saved. One thing is certain, however: we do know quite a bit about Adam despite the paucity of the available evidence.

CONCLUSION

Adam is being presented in this book as a real man who was created on day 6 of a 6-day Creation period. He is a man whose life carries so many theological and spiritual overtones that to ignore him is to be spiritally naïve. It is necessary to come to a conclusion about him if one wishes to claim to be a fully autonomous spiritual person. The decisions we make will affect our lives since they will underpin our personal ideologies which govern the actions of our lives. Adam is not just a piece of knowledge or even a piece of misinformation; Adam is central to our lives as Christians, as we will see.

These pages are designed to make us think clearly about the claims made for Adam; to ask the question "Why believe in Adam?" and to show the logic of saying, "I believe in Adam".

Chapter One

FAITH'S RATIONALITY

'When reason's ray shines over all
And puts the saints to rout:
Then Peter's holiness will pall,
And Paul's will peter out.'

This amusing doggerel is making the obvious point that as reason increases so faith decreases in men's minds, since faith and reason are supposed to be at opposite ends of the intellectual spectrum. Many philosophers seem to have struggled to increase reason and rationality in an attempt to eliminate the need for religious faith. What such men seem to fail to recognize is that faith is not opposed to reason. It may be, as Hebrews puts it,

'the assurance of things hoped for,
the conviction of things not seen,' (Heb. 11:1),

but that does not make it irrational, based on nothing more than a wish-fulfilment. True faith is not a leap in the dark at all, it is founded firmly in solid evidence which can easily be assessed on rational criteria and under the strictest rules of logic. A faith which cannot withstand the searing heat of rational logic is not *true* faith at all, and, no matter how successfully one can build subsequent belief systems from its unqualified axioms, it will always be no more stable than a house of cards, ready to fall at the slightest wind or the mildest shaking of its foundations. It is the theory of Evolution which I believe is a house of cards and therefore an irrational faith-system, not belief in Adam and the Christian faith.

Nevertheless it is true to say that as man has applied his reason to the phenomena of the existence of life and has seemed to find his answers in science, so the Christian faith has appeared to totter and has lost its appeal in the minds of the populace as a whole. Even people who cling to their Christian faith, when it comes to the message of salvation in Jesus, have often felt it necessary to jettison their belief in Adam as a result of this modern scientific onslaught.

It may be unfair to expect the non-religious world to believe in Adam but, amongst those who claim some sort of Christian faith, the majority would also probably declare that Adam was not a literal figure either. A belief in a literal Adam admittedly poses problems at the scientific level for the Christian but to deny Adam pulls the theological rug from under the Christian's feet and, to mix the metaphor quite deliberately, the house falls like a house of cards in a gentle breeze. There no longer remains a logically consistent account of sin, evil, the need of a Saviour and indeed of the existence of God. A belief in Adam is crucial to so many topics of vital concern in the world today that to eliminate him to satisfy the scientists has grave consequences at both the spiritual and the physical level.

It is not my concern here to present the 'scientific' case against Evolution nor to address myself to the theological possibilities of a Creationist/Catastrophist view of earth history. This has been done elsewhere.[1] What I want to do is give careful thought to the implications behind the notion that Adam was a literal figure who lived in a literal Eden with Eve, his wife, and that the biblical stories found in Genesis 1-11 (Creation to Babel) are not myth (religious or otherwise[2]) but are historical fact.

THE 'DEATH' OF ADAM

Two hundred years ago Adam was still very much 'alive' in men's minds. Few questioned his existence as a literal person because no seemingly rational case against him had been presented. To accept a literal Adam cannot be done in isolation because Adam comes as a theological package which has Christ at its centre. It is a case of 'love me: love my dog' for the two go together and are inseparable. To believe in Adam is to accept the biblical account of the formation of the world, the origin of sin, the nature of evil and God's answer — in Christ — for dealing with it; and the reverse is equally the case. If one accepts the biblical account of salvation in Christ, one accepts the biblical account of the origin and nature of sin and its remedy, which includes Adam at source.

But independence and rebellion have been human characteristics we all seem to have inherited from Adam. It seems to be an empirical fact that, given half a chance, most people will prefer to live their lives as if God did not exist. A theory which can effectively eliminate Him from their calculations takes on an added aura and is seized on with uncritical alacrity.

The irony of the situation is that it was men of strong religious convictions, who were seeking to probe the mysteries of the Creation in order to reveal the might and majesty of God, who paved the way for the theories which began by reducing the Creator to little more than a master mechanic and ended by making Him totally redundant. The laws of celestial mechanics discovered by men like Kepler and Newton are a case in point. They pioneered the path which led to the acceptance of the concepts of uniformitarianism and gradualism, exemplified in the geological axiom 'the present is the key to the past' and which spawned modern geology, biology, physics and astronomy.

Evolution as a concept was not new in the mid-19th century when it became popular. The ancient Greeks had postulated it and men with atheistic tendencies down the years had tried, unsuccessfully, to popularize it. It was Darwin's, *The Origin of Species* (1859) which legitimized these loose, independent ideas by presenting the world with a unifying theory of evolutionary origins.

As a theory it has little to commend it scientifically since it is both unfalsifiable and untestable, nor does it fit the observable facts, save in a vague way, or the proven laws of science[3]. Nevertheless Evolution ousted Adam as an explanation of biological origins because of its philosophical acceptability. Men often seem incapable of delighting to live their lives believing in an Almighty Creator God, preferring to appear to be more rational (and therefore more open minded) than those who avowedly live by faith. Evolutionists frequently fail to recognize that they too are living by faith of 'the assurance of things hoped for, the conviction of things not seen'. The missing links in their evolutionary chains persistently fail to be found and fossil species stubbornly refuse to mutate over countless millennia remaining intact with just small variations present to excite their evolutionary devotees. Moths, birds, fish and horses, so frequently cited as evidence for Evolution, do indeed change their varieties under natural selection; and may even become separate species when kept in isolation (e.g. on a remote island), but for some annoying reason they still remain recognizeable as moths, birds, fish and horses. The hoped-for developments are quite frankly not seen and many scientists today acknowledge this truth hence their changing position from gradualism to a punctuated process in Evolution; at the time of writing. The 'step' theory is replacing the 'slope' theory but the basic concept is still retained with an almost religious fervour; a fact too which is being recognized within its ranks[4].

A hundred and thirty odd years ago Christian believers crumpled swiftly after Darwin had turned Adam into a 'mythological' character in order to accommodate the new radical views of science. Noble explanations such as the frequently held view that 'science and religion do not compete but provide different perspectives on the same theme,' are heard. 'Science deals with the material and religion with the spiritual' is another popular view, as if man is divisible into two separate and independent halves which can co-exist in perfect discord within the breast of the Christian believer. Well could it be said that these people who peddle(d) such views are more concerned with the praise of men than the truth of God. When Adam 'died', faith nose-dived as a result.

This was the start of the theological decline which characterized the latter half of the 19th century and the first half of the 20th century. It is frequently called 'liberalism' by 'conservatives' and 'progressivism' by 'liberals'. From questioning the literal truth of Adam and Genesis 1-11, these scholars moved into questioning the authorship of the Pentateuch and declared that men called P, J and E have taken over from Moses; Isaiah only wrote part of 'Isaiah'; Paul could not possibly have written Ephesians, Timothy and Titus; and the Synoptic Gospels owe their origin to documents Q, L and M instead of Matthew, Mark and Luke. 'Form Criticism' and 'Redaction Criticism' have reduced the Gospels to pulp and the Bible, after their treatment, has become the most unreliable, uninspired book ever to be foisted onto a gullible public; or so they lead us to believe. The Bible will survive; the gates of liberal scholarship will not prevail against it. But by the early 1960's, just 100 years after Darwin, there was the feeling in many theological circles that 'God is Dead'.

Adam died *circa* 1860 and God followed him a century later!

THE RATIONALE OF FAITH

We mentioned at the beginning that true faith must not be merely a wish-fulfilment but must be founded in a logical rationale. Such a rationale must be capable of the most intense scrutiny which people, with a commitment to searching for truth, can investigate with as great an incisiveness as any prosecuting counsel at a murder trial.

The Christian faith is the one major belief-system which bares its soul to its inner-most depths and challenges sceptics to make a diagnosis. This statement is not necessarily true of all sub-systems (denominations) within the orthodox umbrella title of 'Christianity', many of whom fly shy of such an examination, being content to pronounce as if by Divine fiat. Be that as it may, the Christianity I am referring to is the faith 'once for all revealed to the saints' (Jude 3), namely the faith revealed exclusively in the New Testament with no frills or subsequent surgery used to effect a more cosmetically acceptable visage. I am interested not in 'religiosity' nor in 'churchianity' (both of which appear to be the cause of much of the sceptical rejection of Christianity) but in the exemplar as laid out in the documents we now call the New Testament. This is not, however, a difficult job since the rationale of Christianity is not a number of diverse, unqualifiable, unquestionable axioms of belief; it hinges on one single truth-claim namely the resurrection of Jesus of Nazareth.

The unfolding message of the Bible is that it may physically begin with Adam but it hinges on the truth of the resurrection. This is the claim that there was a man called Jesus, who lived nearly 2000 years ago in a small country virtually the size of Wales, in an insignificant village of that country away from the metropolis of Jerusalem. That at the age of thirty He began to teach and that He made claims to being God-with-us and did miracles to prove it, is also affirmed. The former claim got Him into hot water with the authorities who decided He was a blasphemer and consequently had Him put to death on a cross some three years or so after He first began to make His claims. This much is rarely in dispute. Most biblical critics agree that there was such a man who taught truths and who was put to death under Pontius Pilate. Thus the Christian claim is not based on an idea or on a philosophy but in the historical reality of the life of this man.

He died a horrible death and was laid to rest in a tomb. Because of the claims He made and the supposed fanaticism of His followers, guards were placed on His tomb to prevent His body being stolen. Nevertheless three days after He died His body was missing and was never discovered. His followers claimed He rose from the dead and that this resurrection proved His claims to be true. Ever since that day all of His subsequent followers have proclaimed this as a fact. The question is,"Is it a fact?".

The rationale of Christianity is based solidly in an event not an idea. An event can be put under the critical microscope of historical investigation and can be interpreted logically and rationally. It matters not a whit what we believe in our hearts, it is what our heads tell us, as a result of our honest inquiry, which must count. But it matters a great deal how we react to the results of that investigation for if our investigation reveals that this dead man actually did rise from the dead then He was no ordinary man, nor were His teachings merely great human wisdom. His resurrection, if true, confirms the truth-claims made for Him as being true and make His other words authoritative too. The truth about Adam becomes a question of authority.

Christians are people who accept that the only rational explanation for that empty tomb and the disappearance of the body is that He rose. The fact that nobody had ever done that unaided before, or since, and that it was or would be a unique event, does not militate against it. If He was God-with-us, we would expect to find Him to be a unique man, who lived a unique life, who taught unique truth and who had unique elements surrounding His departure from the scene of this world. We would also find it not too difficult to accept that such a man had a unique birth and had powers which went well beyond those claimed for others who were just wonder workers. One wonders just what sort of a God people, who find the miraculous claims for and about Jesus to be anathema, would want if they could mould Him in their image. The accounts of the life and death of Jesus are absolutely consistent with His claims or the claims made for Him. But are they true? Whether we say "Yes" or "No" we must agree that something unique certainly happened.

ASSESSING THE CLAIMS

A careful examination of the claims and counter-claims concerning the death of Jesus will show that the only serious argument, which can be put up against His having been resurrected, is that such an event would go against all naturalistic explanations and is unfalsifiable or unverifiable since it was a unique event. Nobody saw it and it has never been repeated nor can one conduct an experiment to test it to see if it is possible. The case rests on argument and not on experiment, therefore it is all circumstantial evidence based on probability which must decide the issue. Hence this leaves it up to the individual to assess the claims and decide on His own verdict. This may mean faith but it is a far cry from being irrational faith. The claim that 'Jesus rose' is not an appeal to the heart (though it makes an appeal there too) but to the head.[5]

Where all other considerations fail the one which remains intact, no matter how implausible it may appear to us, must be the one we accept. It was never claimed that Jesus was an ordinary man. If He was, as is claimed, God-with-us, then a unique death would be perfectly consistent with a unique life. Christianity is neither inconsistent, incoherent nor irrational and can, and has, faced the onslaught of atheistic secularism down nearly 2000 years. On this the head can and must rule the heart. Once it succeeds then truth will out. It is when the heart rules the head that truth gets blurred.

The Resurrection of Jesus is the rationale of faith.

CONSEQUENCES OF THE RESURRECTION BEING TRUE

The consequences of the claim about Jesus' death and resurrection being true are enormous. Such a view can never leave us with a 'take-it-or-leave-it' attitude. To rise from the dead makes His claims to authority to be true. This not only authenticates the writing of the Scriptures it indicates that He was not bound in the vice-like grip of the thought-processes of His day. When He argued about divorce He referred back to Eden (Mtt. 19:3-9): when He pointed to the end of the world He referred back to Noah (Mtt.24:36-39). There was no doubt in His mind that Moses wrote a goodly and authoritative part of the Bible (Luke 16:29-31), and that such events were not only real but were also laden with deep spiritual significance.

The spiritual significance of the first eleven chapters of Genesis cannot be overstated. They contain the key to the Scriptures, for within their pages lies the biblical explanation of the origin of sin and its consequences, which were physical as well as spiritual, and issues of obedience with its consequent bedfellows of judgement and salvation. At rock bottom, all religions attempt to provide answers to the problem of evil, pain and suffering. That is their *raison d'être* and in Christianity lies the most amazing 'answer' of all. It can only be incredibly true or an amazing hoax. It can never be a useful religious myth.

Christianity clearly teaches that Jesus came to restore what Adam lost. If Adam never existed then, equally clearly, he could not have lost anything so Jesus' mission was merely chasing the wind or trying to grasp a rainbow. The message of Jesus makes no sense without Adam. If nature was not once 'red in tooth and claw' but became thus as a result of sin, then the message of Jesus makes sense. If nature was always the same, then the gospel *is* pointless and Jesus came to rectify something which had never gone wrong. Nature would then be simply enacting its preprogrammed rôle, moving to some unguided utopia with a mindless lack of haste.

These themes will be developed as we go through the book. It will be seen that with a firm belief in Adam no theological gymnastics are necessary when confronting the major issues of life. Without him many are left floundering in a whirlpool of doubt and even the straws at which they clutch are mere shadows of what they hope may be true.

It takes a lot more faith not to believe in Adam yet still sustain a belief in God and Jesus. Unfortunately so many people lose their faith as a result of the attacks made on it. It is not for nothing that we live in an increasingly secular society for, when the bedrock of religious faith is removed, the house crumbles. It will be seen that a belief in Adam is not naïve; it is in fact the most satisfying way of interpreting the problems of life.

That is why I believe in Adam.

NOTES.

[1] Fisher G.A., *Speak Through the Earthquake, Wind and Fire,* Countyvise, 1982.

[2] A religious myth is not neccessarily an untrue fictitious story. It is a story which, it is claimed, can be either true or false but which contains great spiritual truth and teaching.

[3] For example, the theory of evolution violates the Second Law of Thermodynamics. Briefly this teaches that the universe is running down, going colder and moving from order to chaos. This is called 'entropy' and entropy is increasing not decreasing.

[4] Midgley Mary, *Evolution as a Religion,* Methuen, 1985 and Denton M. *Evolution: A Theory in Crisis* Burnet Books, 1988.

[5] See Morison F., *Who Moved the Stone?,* Faber, 1930.

Chapter Two

IN THE BEGINNING GOD

THE GREAT QUESTION

Men have always been interested in probing back to their origins, either of their family, nation, race, mankind itself, the world or the Universe. As scientists look deeper into space they believe they are looking further back in time[1], and the more distant a galaxy they discover the more excited those become to whom the question of genesis is of vital importance. There are many great questions about origins still to be asked and which are being asked at all levels.

It was Jesus who, quoting Psalm 8:2, popularized the words, "Out of the mouth of babes and sucklings," (Mtt. 21:16) which means that children can sometimes see truth with a clarity not given to adults. In His case they 'saw' His messianic claims as being true; but children are quite capable of asking profound questions which go far beyond the level of "how long is a piece of string?"[2], even to asking, "What is white?" or, "What is love?".

A teacher, especially a teacher of Religious Knowledge, faces the question, "Who made God?", many times a year. When I was a teacher, many of my questioners asked from a sense of genuine enquiry but equally some were clever enough to believe that they had somehow trapped me. To them this is the ultimate question and they feel smug that they have been smart enough to think it out. Of course, it is a non-question and that fact is very easy to demonstrate. My reply usually went something like this:

> "That is really a pointless question because if I could give you an answer you would then ask, "Who made the person who made God?", and if I could answer that, you would say again, "Who made the person who made the person who made God?". You can go on and on forever along that route and get nowhere because it is an infinite regression. You soon realize that you have come to a person who began it all and who was not made but always existed. We call Him 'God' and that's part of what we mean by 'God'; somebody who always existed."

This seemed to satisfy my pupils, if they could understand it, but what they did not know is that they had just been taught one of the four, so-called, 'proofs' for the existence of God; the *cosmological proof.*[3]

The Bible makes no concessions to atheism or agnosticism in its treatment of God. The opening verse presupposes the existence of God and from Genesis to Revelation no case is argued. The nearest it comes is a statement in Hebrews 11:6, "For whoever would draw near to God must believe that he exists and that he rewards those who seek him", but it would be safe to say that the unbeliever could just as easily substitute the word 'fairies' for 'God' and declare that in order to 'see' them and 'know' them you must believe in them otherwise they will never reveal themselves. If you do not 'believe', then you will never 'see': and that sounds like the sorts of arguments which are so often presented by Christians to a sceptical, disbelieving world.

Of course this would be a spurious substitution because there is no evidence for the existence of fairies but there are plenty of pointers to the existence of God. The Psalmist declares, 'The heavens are telling the glory of God; and the firmament proclaims his handiwork', (Ps. 19:1) and Paul argues from Creation to God in Romans 1.

'For what can be known about God is plain to them (the Gentiles), because God has shown it to them. Ever since the creation of the world his invisible nature, namely, his eternal power and deity, has been clearly perceived in the things that have been made' (Rom. 1:19-20, brackets mine).

This is as close to the *teleological 'proof'* of the existence of God as the Bible comes, the argument from design and purpose, and is the only one of the four traditional 'proofs' to get a small airing let alone full-blown treatment.

When modern man examines the world in which he lives, he recognizes two main facts: (a) everything is the result of cause and effect, (b) there seems to be a pattern or design to the world. The original scientists who introduced the modern scientific age, men like Kepler, Copernicus and Newton, firmly believed that an **examination of the physical world and Universe would reveal the glory of Creation and the mind of the Creator.** They were so convinced that God had made the world and that in making it He made it knowable and understandable, that they looked for design and the laws which would explain the patterns they discovered. Once they had explained them they were able to predict the Universe in ways impossible before. The way, however, was then opened for an understanding only of a God of design, a mechanistic God, who was little more than a master mechanic who set the machinery in motion and who now watches it work; anything more is beyond the scope of science. This 'deist' God was quickly seized upon by intellectuals in the 18th century but before long He too was found to be redundant; so the conviction that there is pattern and plan in the Universe persists to this day in the scientific world but the idea that there is a designer and a purpose to it all has largely vanished. The scientist today searches passionately for patterns and universal laws and then seeks to make connections but leaves purposes (and God) largely to the theologian.

In seeking to explain origins today the scientist turns to modern examples of cause and effect and then extrapolates back in time. He knows that for every observable effect there is a cause, but no matter how far back in time he pushes his 'cause' he comes to the point at which he, like the Christian, must accept the eternal existence of something, which in his case if he does not believe in God, is some sort of matter or gravity wave. The unbelieving scientist can rightly argue that in seeking ultimate answers the Christian can only move one stage further back in the chain of cause and effect and his argument for a God, who is eternally existent and uncreated, is no more logical or valid than the scientist's claim for eternally existing matter. He just chooses to stop one stage ahead of the believer. He would also argue that his belief in pattern does not presuppose a designer at all but just springs from what is observed. If evidence of design does presuppose a designer, why should it be one only and not many; why does it argue for monotheism as opposed to polytheism? Modern designed projects frequently have a design team, so why did the Universe not have one too? Thus the cosmological and teleological arguments 'prove' nothing much about the existence or otherwise of God let alone that there is a purpose behind it all.

MODERN MAN'S DESPAIR

When viewing the Universe, the unbelieving scientist probably can take comfort in his formulae and work, but a man like Mark Twain, who took little or no comfort in his work or philosophy, on coming to a sad, tragic old age, could only view God and the world from a position of total despair. The conclusion of his posthumously published short story, 'The Mysterious Stranger', written when his private world lay in tatters around him, is:

' *"Life itself is only a vision, a dream"*.

' "Strange! that you should not have suspected years ago — centuries, ages, eons ago! — for you have existed, companionless, through all the eternities. Strange indeed, that you should not have suspected that your universe and its contents were only dreams, visions, fiction! Strange, because they are so frankly and hysterically insane — like all dreams: a God who could make good children as easily as bad, yet preferred to make bad ones; who could have made every one of them happy, yet never made a single happy one; who made them prize their bitter life, yet stingily cut it short; who gave his angels eternal happiness unearned, yet required his other children to earn it: who gave his angels painless lives, yet cursed his other children with biting miseries and maladies of mind and body; who mouths justice and invented hell — mouths mercy and invented hell — mouths Golden Rules, and forgiveness multiplied by seventy times seven, and invented hell; who mouths morals to other people and has none himself; who frowns upon crimes, yet commits them all; who created man without invitation, then tries to shuffle the responsibility for man's acts upon man, instead of honorably placing it where it belongs, upon himself; and finally, with altogether divine obtuseness, invites this poor, abused slave to worship him! . . .

' "You perceive, *now* that these things are all impossible except in a dream. You perceive that they are pure and puerile insanities, the silly creations of an imagination that is not conscious of its freaks — in a word, that they are a dream, and you the maker of it. The dream-marks are all present: you should have recognized them earlier.

' "It is true, that which I have revealed to you: there is no God, no universe, no human race, no earthly life, no heaven, no hell. It is all a dream — a grotesque and foolish dream. Nothing exists but you. And you are but a *thought* — a vagrant thought, a useless thought, a homeless thought, wandering forlorn among the empty eternities!" '[4]

Complete hopelessness is sad but there is a fierce logic to it at a superficial level. This passage has been quoted here at length because Twain made many points which will be taken up later on. But let it be said here and now that a biblical understanding of the perfection of Creation, Adam and the Fall would have helped him to find some of his answers. However even this cannot and will not satisfy unless the true key to unlocking the mysteries of God, Jesus Christ and His resurrection, is understood and appreciated.

The question of deity is solved then, not in traditional proofs, but in the resurrection of Jesus. In the resurrection lies the key to the Scriptures, the key to life and key to God. If Christ is not raised, our faith is in vain and I would feel happy to agree that there is no God. But if Christ is risen, the question concerning the existence of God is answered affirmatively. No other power could achieve that. Life then is not a meaningless dream but has a Divine purpose, however imperfectly that purpose is perceived.

WHAT KIND OF GOD?

If it is conceded that there is a God, it is important to decide what kind of a God He is. In his book, *Evil, Suffering and Religion,* Brian Hebblethwaite makes the point when dealing with that topic, 'it is not only the fact of belief in God that makes the difference. It also depends on what sort of God you believe in', (p.98). This is true no matter what subject is under discussion. There are so many views of deity represented in the theistic religions that it is important to realize that our own image of God creates our own problems when tackling theological issues.

There are the obvious stereotypes in men's minds from God being like a benevolent grandfather who is indulgent to our self-centredness, through the stern judge who is counting our sins and will one day wreak vengeance on us, to the disinterested master mechanic who set the wheels in motion and now watches the inevitable outworkings of His Creation with a detached indifference. The Christian carries with him an image of God as 'Abba' Father (or Dad) who is love but before whom men should be reverent and recognize that, though emminently approachable, He is still holy.

These beliefs however are not important to the topics under discussion here. The things needed to be considered are questions concerning His power (omnipotence), knowledge (omniscience), involvement in the world (omnipresence), and how such a God can help us with an understanding of the issues raised.

GOD'S POWER

It is important to have a very clear idea of the power of God. Some religions view God as merely a force for good as opposed to the Devil who is an equal force for evil. Though believing that the two are equal (or nearly so), most believe that one day the good will triumph. God is not viewed in their schemes as being in total control at the moment. This helps them with questions of evil and suffering but denies the biblical view that God is in full control even over Satan.

At the other extreme many people feel that, ever since Gabriel told Mary ' "For with God nothing will be impossible" ' (Luke 1:37), all that believers have to do is to add the words 'God can' to any statement, no matter how illogical, and it comes within the realm of possibility. C.S. Lewis makes this point with his usual lucidity in *The Problem of Pain,* that that which is logically impossible remains impossible even to God. This does not mean that God therefore is not all powerful. Even God cannot make $2+2=5$ or put a physically square peg into a physically round hole and not leave any gaps. On the other hand caution must be exercised by men when they declare what is in their eyes impossible, it may just be that it is their knowledge which is deficient at the time. Later on this seeming limit to God's power will be significant in our discussion of free-will, pain and suffering.

Much as it is important to recognize that there can be limitations imposed on the definition of omnipotence and yet for God to still be fully all powerful, we must not restrict Him to the limits of our understanding. When it comes to the question of Creation it may be natural to say that the Universe has evolved over 15,000,000,000 years but with God it would not be impossible for Him to create a Universe in 6 seconds, 6 minutes, 6 days, or 6,000,000,000 years. The question is not 'could God do it in x time?' but *'did He do it in x time?'*

It is not logically impossible for an omnipotent Creator to choose His own time-scale for His Creation and men must not presumptuously restrict Him to any of their choosing. To do this would presuppose that we know the limitations of the creating process today; yet it is true to say that scientists are constantly discovering and developing in their generation, knowledge which previous generations would have declared to be absolutely impossible. Whilst this is admittedly on a totally different scale of magnitude to anything approaching Creation, the point is still valid. If God did make the world in six days in its total fulness, man may never be able to provide an explanation as to how He did it. We must not make our God and His power too small.

The problem over God's omnipotence lies not in the fact of His power but in how He uses it and demonstrates it.

GOD'S KNOWLEDGE

By definition God is omniscient, which means He knows our thoughts and desires even better than we do ourselves. He knows how many hairs we have on our heads (Mtt. 10:30), and what is more, it is apparently important to Him to have such knowledge. We have noted that to say that God is all powerful does not imply that there are no limitations (maybe self imposed) on Him (cf. Heb. 6:13-20). Could there then be any limits to His knowledge?

Once again any seeming limitations may be man-imposed rather than God-imposed. They may be more the result of our misunderstandings than any deficiency in the Almighty. It is man's view of God which is too small. For example, it is common to talk of 'The Divine Plan' for the world or for our lives and, taken to its extreme, there is a belief in some religious circles that, from cradle to grave, our lives have been mapped out by God in eternity past. Even your reading this book at this precise second was destined before the world began!

To believe that God can only and could only prepare and foreknow one plan is to place an unnecessary limit on His knowledge and one which exists solely in our minds. I could play the world chess champion in a thousand games and the result each time would be inevitable but he could not predict the pattern of the game from start to finish because his play would depend on mine. No analogy is perfect but, within its limitations, this one has its uses on such topics. There is no need for God to impose a single 'play' on mankind's 'game' though the outcome is inevitable. He can allow for us to exercise our free choice, to make our own game, yet still bring it to an inevitable conclusion. To do this implies that God is active in the world and is not a passive spectator.

GOD'S INVOLVEMENT IN THE WORLD

The Christian's God is not seen as being a remote master mechanic nor an equal dualistic force for good alongside evil. This presents the Christian with as many theological problems as it solves and it brings as much discomfort as comfort. The persistent message of the Bible in both testaments is that God is interested and active in His world and such is His involvement, the New Testament asserts, that He came down actively as a human being and identified with His Creation. It is therefore total commitment to the world in the fullest sense that is revealed about God in the Scripture.

This brings comfort and blessing to the Christian who knows that Jesus is able 'to sympathize with our weaknesses' and He cares enough to count our hairs. However such a God also knows our inner heart, our real motives, our secret sins and vices. It would be nice to have a God who was like a benevolent grandfather over whose eyes we could pull the spiritual wool whenever we choose; but we cannot!

Similarly, if God is everywhere and is actively part of the world, the question to be asked is 'why does He not intervene to save people from harm?' How does He opt in and out of our lives? The deist God is remote and brings no comfort or discomfort but allows men to work out their own salvation without His help; the pantheistic God pervades all nature but more as a life-force than monotheistic omnipotence; but neither concept of God troubles the theologian as the Christian concept does.

Like it or not, the biblical God is all-powerful, all knowing and ever present. It does matter what kind of God we believe in. We might well view life as a horrible dream at times. It might be convenient to select the kind of God we want to worship or to reject a belief in a God at all, but many of the problems concerning God, as we shall see, are created by men who reject the first eleven chapters of Genesis as literal truth. Within these chapters there is so much revealed about God and His world that to throw out Adam is to throw out God's theological baby with the theological bathwater.

NOTES

[1] Galactic distances are measured in light years i.e. the distance light can travel in one year at 186,000 miles per second approximately. Thus a star whose distance is calculated at, say, 100,000 light years is being viewed on Earth as it was 100,000 years ago (in theory at least).

[2] The usual answer is 'twice the length of half of it'!

[3] The four 'proofs' are (i) cosmological (cause and effect), (ii) teleological (design and purpose), (iii) ontological (notions of perfection), (iv) moral.

[4] This theory of Twain's is known as 'solipsism'.

Chapter Three

GOD CREATED

A belief in a literal Adam implies a general acceptance of the Genesis account of Creation. It also implies an acceptance of the biblical statements concerning Creation from the other parts of the Scriptures. Such a belief has much to say about the nature of God and His purposes in Creation, spirit beings like angels and demons, and the importance of man and the Earth to God. To reduce the Creation/Evolution debate to questions of 'How?' to the exclusion of 'Why?' is to miss the better half of the problem!

If a belief in Adam is rejected, then it becomes infinitely harder to sustain a theology which accepts a Divine plan for the world, Divine purpose in Creation, the worth of man and his superiority in God's scheme, and the reality of the spirit world. It is not too hard to see that such a rejection must have a significant effect on one's Christology and the great questions of the reality of heaven, hell and salvation.

THE WORLD WHICH GOD CREATED

The Genesis record tells us that at the end of the sixth day of Creation, 'God saw everything that he had made, and behold, it was very good,' (Gen. 1:31). Twain's diatribe against God's Creation, quoted in chapter two, failed to grasp this fundamental point. He said 'a God who could make good children as easily as bad, yet preferred to make bad ones, who could have made every one of them happy, yet never made a single happy one,' shows that he, at least, did not believe in Adam. He goes on then about angels and the unfairness of their creation as opposed to man's. We will look at this a little later on.

A belief in Adam teaches that the whole Creation *was* made perfect, and this must also have included Satan. There was no sin, no fallen angels, no fallen man, no disease, death and corruption; presumably too the Second Law of Thermodynamics was not operating.[1] God created an idyllic paradise with man and not angels as the pinnacle of it all. How long it lasted thus we are not told but it was never God's intention that it should or must go wrong.

Jettison Genesis and one can see very little point in Creation, let alone make a consistent theodicy about the goodness of God. If Evolution is true, God not only preferred to make bad men, He preferred to make a world which could only survive on killing and pain as Nature[2] selected the fittest and killed off the weak.

THE NATURE OF THE DIVINE

Genesis opens with the famous line 'In the beginning God created,' and the apostle John, in an equally famous opening, writes,

'In the beginning was the Word, and the Word was with God, and the Word was God. He was in the beginning with God; all things were made through him, and without him was not anything made that was made,' (John 1:1-3).

Thus, when Genesis declares that God made the world, John declares that it was the Word, 'who became flesh and dwelt among us' as Jesus, who was the agent in Creation. *Jesus made the World!*

Scripture unfolds some of the mystery of the nature of the Divine. If we could understand all that is involved in the Divine, one of two things would be true; either man would be as great as God or God would be no greater than man. Nobody will ever be able to plumb the depths of the nature of the Trinity (or Triunity as some prefer to call it) of the Godhead. From Genesis 1:26 where God said, ' "Let us make man in our image, after our likeness," ' the mystery begins to unfold. God thought of Himself as a plurality and is thus revealed in later Scriptures, especially in the New Testament.

Attempts have been made to present helpful analogies to explain this mystery to simpler minds. Some have suggested that water in its three forms of ice, liquid, and steam would present the ideas of a single substance with a three-part nature to explain the Father, Son and Holy Spirit, which is the inspired revelation to mankind by God Himself concerning His nature. This does not work because a single droplet of water cannot exist as ice, liquid and steam simultaneously, yet the Father, Son and Holy Spirit do.

There is an abstract concept of three functions which go into the composition of every human being, which gets a little nearer to the truth than ice, liquid and steam. This is the three separate but inextricably linked functions we call thinking, feeling and willing. Each is a recognizable individual process, yet they can only operate as or in a single unit. We all know what it is to think, to feel and to will but whatever we think depends on what we feel and will and the same is true of the other two.

What the Bible does reveal is that God has three separate yet linked, aspects to His nature; the Father, who plans everything; the Son, who is the agent, the doer of the Father's will — the one who carries out the Father's plans — ; and the Holy Spirit, who sustains the work, planned by the Father and executed by the Son.

Thus, in Creation the Father planned it, the Son did the work and the Holy Spirit keeps it running (if one can use such terms without being flippant or disrespectful to Him). Similarly when it came to salvation it was the Father's will which the Son carried out and left the Holy Spirit to sustain. The Word, Jesus, had to come to die for us, for to refuse to do so would have meant He denied Himself, and God cannot do that.

DECISIONS IN ETERNITY PAST

The oxymoron 'eternity past' is used as a subtitle to indicate the time before Creation or 'before the foundation of the world', when God laid His plans for the sort of Creation He wanted. The decisions He made at that 'time' were so tremendous that they reveal some wonderful truth about the sort of love God has and what He wants to give us. It also shows just what man threw away when he sinned.

Probably the most quoted verse in the whole Bible is John 3:16 'For God so loved the world that he gave his only Son, that whoever believes in him, should not perish but have eternal life.' God's love for the world and His creatures did not occur some time after the Fall or even just a few years before Jesus was born; His love was there in eternity past for it was before the world was formed that the decision to send Jesus to Calvary was made. As the hymnwriter said:- 'And was there then no other way For God to take? I cannot say.'

It may seem somewhat bizarre to us to imagine God planning the Cross before He had even made the world but this seems to be the case.[3] Not only that, He also planned to save all Christians.[4] He planned the church[5] as the bride of Christ and He planned to defeat Satan finally at the end of time. It is a sign of His omnipotence that He does not crush all opposition, for that would be to make a U-turn on His policy decisions and would suggest that He makes up His plans to meet spiritual contingencies not anticipated earlier.

If this is the case, it raises two fundamental points both of which will receive fuller treatment later.[6] The first is that if God anticipated or even foreordained the Cross because of man's sin, why then does He blame man, and why did He blame man when it went 'wrong', according to plan? — or as Twain puts it, why is He 'a God who created man without invitation, then (who) tries to shuffle the responsibility for man's acts upon man, instead of honorably placing it where it belongs, upon himself?' The second is that if God anticipated all the pain and evil in the world He was to create, He must have thought it so worthwhile to go ahead that He was prepared to pay that price. He must therefore have a wonderful ultimate ending in mind for us all since, to many human minds, the inevitable suffering of one innocent person is not deemed to be worth the act of Creation.

We mentioned in Chapter two, when considering God's omniscience, that it may be a mistake to restrict God's knowledge to one plan only. God could well have conceived many plans, only one of which necessitated the Cross. To return to the chess-match analogy for a minute; there are limitations placed on the players by the confines of the board and the moves each piece is allowed to make, but within those confines an infinite number of games is possible, including at least one which involves the cleverest play of all — the Queen sacrifice — to bring the game to a successful conclusion. God made a world on which to play His great game and it must be played in a time/space context, but the games possible are infinitely more varied than the infinite chess games (if this technically nonsensical expression can be used for emphasis), one of which at least involved the ultimate sacrifice (Queen sacrifice) of the Cross to bring that 'game' to a successful conclusion. However, just as in chess there are many different games where a Queen sacrifice forces a win, so too there could have been many different games where the Cross became inevitable. This may help us all when trying to probe such ideas as predestination, foreordination and foreknowledge, and to place Adam's sin and Judas' betrayal of Christ in context so that the blame is theirs and not God's. Jesus, the Word, agreed to the Cross as a distinct probability in eternity past and was willing to die to save us but it need not have been an inevitable outcome of Creation. God could genuinely have hoped that sin would not have occurred and could honestly blame Adam for it, but that does not mean that the Cross was an afterthought at any time.[8] It was clearly a decision made in eternity past.

THE COST OF CREATION

No believer would ever doubt that the cost of Creation can only be understood in terms of the Cross. This was the price which God was prepared to pay in order that His Divine purposes for humankind would be fulfilled. The relationship of love that He wants to share with men goes far beyond anything else in all Creation including angels. The bliss that Adam lost and Christ restored, but which we will only appreciate in heaven, must be so wonderful that mere adjectives cannot do it justice or even remotely approach doing it justice. Heaven with God passes all understanding.

The act of Creation cost God His Son. Although it has cost mankind untold miseries down the years it did not leave God Himself untouched either. It is impossible to quantify suffering and some might argue that Jesus did not suffer very long when compared with the starving millions of today, or the Jews in Nazi Germany or even others who died on crosses. (His six hour ordeal was apparently quite swift by crucifixion standards). Paul enlightened the Philippians on the matter when he wrote that 'though he was in the form of God, (he) did not count equality with God a thing to be grasped, but emptied himself, taking the form of a servant being born in the likeness of men' (Phil. 2:6-7). It is easy to reel off these well known, beautiful verses but very difficult to be able to comprehend that sort of cost. The price of sin was not just borne for six hours on the Cross, Christ paid it with a lifetime's suffering. Furthermore, when the Father forsook Him on the Cross, the Son became the first and only person yet to have tasted hell which, put at its simplest, is total separation from God. His physical sufferings may have been relatively short humanly speaking on the Cross but not even Satan knows what total separation from God is like. For the Son to be separated was hell for Him but equally so it was agony for the Father to have to do it.

Creation also cost God in another way too. The God of the Bible is not a magician but a worker. To say that 'he rested on the seventh day from all his work which he had done' (Gen. 2:2) implies an energy output and not a mere clicking of the fingers. God has always been active in His Creation and Genesis indicates a cost to Him in this.

Jesus amply illustrated what is possible here when the woman with a haemorrhage touched Him and was healed. He said, ' "Some one touched me; for I perceive that power has gone forth from me," ' (Lk. 8:46). Creation was a full demonstration of the power of God going forth from Him into that which He was making. Biologists agree that even what we call simple creatures are in fact very complex and beautifully made. God put His whole being into the Universe and gave the Earth His very special attention. Genesis reveals this, but normal scientific theories of origins place the Earth as a chance event which, if God is admitted to have played even an originating rôle, cost Him little more than giving it its initial push. No; God was fully committed to His *work* and the biblical view sustains this thought. Any non-biblical or non-literal view is presented with great problems on this score.

THE CREATION OF THE HEAVENS

Day one of the Genesis story says that the first thing God created was the heavens. Astute biblical students then note that He made the Sun, Moon and stars on Day four and find an immediate problem of interpretation at this point. There need not be because there is the implicit understanding that part of what is meant by 'the heavens' is the heavenly host, which includes angels, archangels, cherubim and seraphim.[9] Just what category of this heavenly host Satan was, is not stated but he is a 'glorious one', as Jude 8-9 indicates. Thus all Creation only had its birth five days before Adam and although 'all the sons of God shouted for joy' (Job 38:7) when 'the foundation of the Earth was laid' (Job 38:4) they did not exist in 'eternity past'. They are as much a part of Creation as was Adam.

Of course in a mechanistic universe there is no need even to postulate the existence of heavenly beings and the spirit world, but the Bible has no doubts at all about it. A belief in Adam cements such ideas and gives a solid foundation to this truth too. So what do we learn about the creation of angels which can help us in our studies?

Twain said that God is a God 'who gave his angels eternal happiness unearned, yet required his other children to earn it; who gave his angels painless lives, yet cursed his other children with biting miseries and maladies of mind and body.' An examination of the biblical facts will reveal a different story.

There seems to be a good case of Divine injustice running through Twain's accusations. The questions could quite rightly be asked 'Is God fair? Has He treated angels more preferentially than He has treated men?'

Whatever the differences may be between angels and men, there appears to be one startling similarity; both were given free will. Twain was wrong because angels were not given 'happiness unearned' — they, like men have the capacity to defy God, and some did. God is a creator not a robot maker, and true Creation involves making His creatures genuinely free so that any love and service they give Him will be genuine too. A little girl may thrill when a doll says, "Mummy I love you," as she presses a button which works a preprogrammed tape, but the illusion soon wears off. If God did not allow men's, or angels', love to spring naturally from within them but could receive it on demand when a button was pressed, then nobody, least of all God, would derive any satisfaction therefrom.

Satan and some angels have rebelled against God and have been destined for hell from that moment. God's condemnation against their rebellion is fierce and final. Whereas He sent His Son to redeem the world He has done nothing to redeem the fallen angels. Christ's blood covers men's sins only.

So why are men given a reprieve, or a chance of a reprieve, when angels are not? Why does God's grace not extend to cover His heavenly host?

Twain was right to point out that there are essential differences between the privileges angels received and men received at Creation. Angels were with God immediately after His first creative act which brought them to life and they witnessed the full power and might of His glory. They dwelt in His presence and served Him and still do, constantly. For an angel to reject God and openly rebel is for 'him' to reject knowing fully the glory of God.

Men, on the other hand, have to accept God positively not knowing His glory, never having seen it. One rejected the pure holiness and splendour of God knowing it fully; the other, man, has to accept in faith what he is taught about the God he serves. Angels see God, men cannot, and when Paul says that we are to judge angels[10] there is a hint there that man's acceptance of God in Christ is truly remarkable. They believe in what they know; we believe in what we cannot know fully. Jesus said to Thomas, ' "Have you believed because you have seen me? Blessed are those who have not seen and yet believe," ' (John 20:29). He established a basis of blessing as God sees it. It takes a great faith to believe in a God whom you can never see. God expected better things from the angels because they knew better.

The one thing men need which angels do not, in their relationship to God, is faith. Angels are immortal and saw God in Creation, fashioning worlds by His Word, making delicate insects and great sea monsters and breathing life into Adam. Men live fleeting lives, do not know or see God's purpose and plans in the same way as angels do; yet in faith they love and serve Him. Faith, 'the assurance of things hoped for, the conviction of things not seen' (Heb 11:1), is the ingredient so necessary and vital to man's relationship to God and so unnecessary to the host of heaven. 'The demons believe — and shudder', James said (2:19). The evil spirits knew who Jesus was whilst He was here on earth[11] and acknowledged Him to be the Son of God. God has always and will always bless faith. Men need it but angels do not.

Salvation only comes through faith, and faith is one thing angels cannot know or understand. This is why there is no salvation offered to the fallen angels. Man, as we have said, rebels against that which he does not fully comprehend and conversely he accepts what he does not fully know. Man's weakness is what commends his love to God for when he loves God it is based on a totally different vision of God. Satan and his angels fell in open rebellion against the holiness, purity, might and majesty of a God they knew and saw. They needed no faith and still do not need faith to believe in God and Jesus as Saviour, consequently there is no salvation for them. Their rebellion was total and complete. It is true to say that, in one sense, they received greater unearned blessings than man in Creation but they also receive the greater condemnation. This reveals that the relationship which God wanted with man was to be on a different basis, one which was forged out of a much more childlike and innocent love based on pure trust.

WHEN WAS THE FALL OF SATAN?

Realizing that on Day six God's Creation was declared to be 'very good' raises questions as to what was Satan's sin and when did he commit it? Jesus said, ' "He was a murderer from the beginning and has nothing to do with the truth because there is no truth in him. When he lies, he speaks according to his own nature for he is a liar and the father of lies," ' (John 8:44). The Devil did not sin until after God had pronounced His Creation very good and it may be presumptuous to speculate further but there is a consistency in the thought that his tempting Eve was his initial act of rebellion. The Fall was in fact the fall of Satan and men together.

If Satan was not created on Day one but fell before the world was made, God must have created a created being before He began to create, which is nonsense and also God's completed Creation never was very good at all. No, his rebellion was as he turned man's heart against God; away from the Creator.

Isaiah, talking about the sin of the king of Babylon seems to give a picture of the nature of Satan's sin:—

> 'How you are fallen from heaven O Day Star, son of Dawn! How you are cut down to the ground, you who laid the nations low! You said in your heart, 'I will ascend to heaven; above the stars of God I will set my throne on high; I will sit on the mount of assembly in the far north; I will ascend above the heights of the clouds, I will make myself like the Most High.' (Is. 14:12-14)

It is difficult to imagine any king literally thinking that he could make himself 'like the Most High' but Satan could easily have done so.[12] The only way he could fulfil this ambition was through man. The Devil cannot create worlds of his own so he could only hope to control the one which God had created as precious and pure for His glory. To win men's love from God was the only way Satan could truly rebel. Thus the Earth became the setting for the spiritual battle between God and Satan. Hence Jesus had to come to Earth to gain the victory. Satan has no kingdom apart from the world. He is destroyed when the world is destroyed.

The question could be posed as to how Satan could be a 'murderer from the beginning' if his initial sin came when he tempted Eve? Whom did he murder? Jesus Himself supplied the answer when, in the Sermon on the Mount He said, ' "You have heard that it was said to the men of old, 'You shall not kill; and whoever kills shall be liable to judgement'. But I say to you that everyone who is angry with his brother shall be liable to judgement," ' (Mtt. 5:21-22). John adds greater clarification to this in his first letter (3:15), 'Anyone who hates his brother is a murderer, and you know that no murderer has eternal life abiding in him.' Anger and hatred are the equivalent to murder in God's eyes. The Devil did not have to murder anybody literally to be called a 'murderer' he just had to hate; and hate he did! He hated God and His Creation and he deliberately set out to destroy it. When Adam and Eve fell Satan had killed them spiritually (though God may well have 'resurrected' them by His grace).

Satan was a murderer though he killed nobody instantly. Poisons can be quick or slow acting but each is as effective. Adam and Eve were poisoned fatally and later died, but in hate at the time of the Fall he corrupted all Creation, thus bringing tragedy to mankind and making the Cross inevitable, though he neither knew nor appreciated that fact. Satan is not omniscient, omnipotent or omnipresent; he is just a created 'glorious one' who also could not look where angels longed to look.[13]

THE CREATION OF MAN

The American writer Robert Penn Warren in his book *All the King's Men* has an interesting passage on the creation of man put into the lips of the real father of the main character:-

> 'The creation of man whom God in His foreknowledge knew doomed to sin was the awful index of God's omnipotence. For it would have been a thing of trifling and contemptible ease for Perfection to create mere

perfection. To do so would, to speak truth, be not creation but extension. Separateness is identity and the only way for God to create, truly create, man was to make him separate from God himself, and to be separate from God is to be sinful. The creation of evil is, therefore, the index of God's glory and His power. That had to be so that the creation of good might be the index of man's glory and power. But by God's help By His help and in His wisdom,' (pages 446-447).

At first glance there seems to be a profound wisdom in that passage. The opening sentences do indeed carry quite a wealth of thinking points. God could have merely created perfection pre-programmed to perfection and each would have been a spiritual, if not a genetic, clone. We have already considered some of the significance of the decision taken by God to create man and the heavenly host knowing that, in the terms of real Creation, it was doomed and the Cross was inevitable.

From here on in, however, the ideas go astray theologically. The omnipotence of God is such that He could truly create separate beings who were perfect. He did not have to create sinfulness in order that man could be separate, what He had to do was to create *the potential* for sin, which is not the same thing.

Creating potential is definitely not the same as creating the effect itself. For example the splitting of the atom was a morally neutral act not in itself responsible for the nuclear bomb. It is true that it made the atom bomb a distinct possibility and that, knowing man's nature, somebody, somewhere and at some time would no doubt use it thus, but the responsibility for the misuse of this power available to mankind lies not with the creator of the potential but with the people who misused it. It could equally have been used as an energy source and in medicine solely for man's benefit.

God created man as a free agent. He gave him free will. This gave man the potential to sin by misusing this freedom in opposing Him. The power of the split atom can be used in peaceful and beneficial ways or it can be used to destroy. Man's will could lead him to love and serve God because man chose so to do or it could be used to oppose God because man chose thus. When Adam misused his freedom his nature fell. Whereas Adam's original inclination was to love God because he was perfect, the fallen man's inclination is to rebel. God could rightly say, even of a righteous man like Noah, that 'the imagination of man's heart is evil from his youth,' (Gen. 8:21); and Paul could write that 'all have sinned and fall short of the glory of God' (Rom. 3:23). It was Adam who sinned and became separate as a result. God could no more create sin than He could tempt anybody,[14] for that would be to deny His nature. It was the creation of man's free will not the creation of evil which made man separate and was the measure of God's omnipotence and the index of His glory and power.

Man was not created to be sinful but rather to have a loving free relationship with God. It was to have been an association of reciprocal love with all of the blessings which such love brings to both parties. God has never stopped loving His Creation. It is man who spoilt it and who can only be restored, as Robert Penn Warren suggested, 'by, God's help. By His help and in His wisdom.'

NOTES

[1] The 2nd Law of Thermodynamics is based on the observed scientific fact that the universe is running down, growing cooler and is becoming more chaotic, i.e. the Universe is subject to decay.

[2] The great substitute word for 'God' in non-Christian thinking.

[3] Revelation 13:8 (AV): Acts 2:23

[4] Romans 8:29-30, 11:2, 1 Peter 1:2,20, Ephesians 1:5,11

[5] Ephesians 1

[6] See pages 46-51.

[7] See B Hebblethwaite — *Evil, Suffering and Religion,* Sheldon Press 1976 page 7

[8] Some teach that the Cross and the Church were never part of God's plans but were substituted when Christ failed to establish an earthly kingdom. This is not so.

[9] The other part of day one's 'heavens' could have been population 2 stars which form the centre of our galaxy. Day 4 saw the Sun, Moon and population 1 stars created.

[10] 1 Corinthians 6:3

[11] Mark 1:24

[12] In Ezekiel 28:11-19 we see the lament over the king of Tyre couched in terms which would fit God's lament over Satan far better.

[13] 1 Peter 1:12

[14] James 1:13-15

Chapter Four

BITING MISERIES

To be perfectly honest most religions have it far easier than Christianity when it comes to the problem of pain and evil. Suffering is the biggest single obstacle in men's minds to accepting the Christian view of God and the world. This fact must be acknowledged, faced full on, and tackled.

It was Augustine of Hippo who formulated the problem in its clearest way. He said,

'Either God cannot abolish evil or He will not; if He cannot, then He is not all-powerful and if He will not, then He is not all-good.'

It is in Christianity that the highest form of the doctrine of God is found and therein lies the trouble. God is declared to be supreme, omnipotent, in full control of all Creation and to be love. 'God is love', John writes (1 John 4:8) and the unapproachable perfection and goodness of the Father is one of the leading messages which Jesus preached. God is 'Abba, Father' to the Christian. We today would call Him 'Dad', reverently of course, and, ' "What man of you, if his son asks for a fish, will give him a serpent? If you then, who are evil, know how to give good gifts to your children, how much more will your Father who is in heaven give good things to those who ask him!" ' (Mtt. 7:9-11). The question then remains: "How can a good, powerful, loving God allow evil and biting miseries to exist on Earth?" The Christian cannot escape the problem or dodge the question.

NON-CHRISTIAN VIEWS

There are many religious views which refuse to offer explanations of evil, pain and suffering at all. They accept it as a fact and simply try to help people to cope with it. Buddhism is a leading example of this approach. Others refuse to accept it as a fact and declare it to be unreal. Some forms of Hinduism adopt this approach.

The Christian Science Church also declares the unreality of evil. Of course, it is neither Christian nor scientific and is a modern version of the Greek gnostic heresy called Docetism. In the Docetic view matter is evil and spirit is good. Thus, since God is spirit and Jesus is the Son of God, He could not have had real flesh; so the argument goes. This reduces Christ's sufferings at Calvary to a sham because His pain only appeared to be real. Moving some stages on, the Christian Scientist declares all pain to be unreal and thus nullifies the reality of Christ's sufferings on the Cross.

Pain is real and evil too. As the limerick poking gentle fun at Christian Science indicates:

'Said a young Christian Scientist from Deal,
"I believe that all pain isn't real.
Yet when pricked by a pin,
Which punctures my skin,
I dislike what I fancy I feel".

To declare the unreality of suffering is really to deny the reliability of the senses. If man cannot believe in the evil things of the world because his senses confuse him, neither can he believe in the good because those same senses which deny evil must also deny good. These philosophies are, as Jude said in denouncing another form of gnostic heresy, 'waterless clouds, carried along by winds; fruitless trees in late autumn, twice dead, uprooted; wild waves of the sea, casting up the foam of their own shame; wandering stars for whom the nether gloom of darkness has been reserved for ever' (Jude 12-13).

Most religions, however, do not deny the existence of biting miseries. On the contrary, it could truly be said they they are obsessed with them. They spend the bulk of their 'spiritual energy' in trying to help their followers cope with the vicissitudes of life. How they do this depends largely on the god or gods in which they believe or, to be more accurate, just how they view the power and attributes of the deities they acknowledge.

Many peoples believe in a multiplicity of deities with equal, or almost equal, powers. Life is seen as a struggle between the forces of good and evil. Most take the optimistic view that the good will triumph in the long run but it is by no means certain. When things go wrong the malevolent forces within the natures of the deities must be placated as they are seen to be the cause of the current evil. Such gods are capricious and act with total inconsistency[1] but it is never too hard for weak-willed human beings to recall some wrong which they have committed and for which they may be being punished when evil befalls them; so they come easily to accept this scenario. Dualism however is not taught in the Judaeo/Christian system of the Bible.

It is the monotheistic religions which feel the pricks of evil most acutely, especially if the one god is viewed as not only being omnipotent (all powerful) but also good. Here the God of Christianity is put under most pressure because Jesus laid emphasis on Him as being a loving Father, as we noted earlier. Jehovah of the Jews and Allah of the Muslims is far more apt to punish and wreak wrath on His enemies than the Father who loves even His enemies!

The Christian not only has to cope with the problems which his view of God presents but also with the apparent dualism in his theodicy. The existence of spiritual forces devoted to evil and epitomized by Satan make it hard to sustain a pure monotheism. To maintain that an omnipotent God has allowed a powerful evil being to oppose Him, may help explain the nature of the cause of evil but it casts questions over the nature of God. On the other hand to deny the reality of the existence of Satan reverses the problem. It makes a consistent theology of God a lot easier but puts us in all sorts of trouble over suffering and God's part in it.

COPING WITHOUT ADAM

The vast majority of the world has to cope without Adam because they have either never heard of him or, having heard, they deny he ever existed. It is to the latter group that we now turn our attention briefly.

People who deny the existence of God and the efficacy of religion have to erect some sort of sociological or psychological system to explain and cope with evil. These schemes are usually bolstered by modern evolutionary theories and can often become 'religions' in themselves.

Communism

It is a well known fact that Karl Marx wanted to dedicate *Das Kapital* to Charles Darwin, because he felt that Darwin had provided the scientific, biological rationale for his sociological and political theories. Marx believed that human evil, at least, could be eliminated once the inequalities of life had been erased. He had a vision of a perfect state where men worked for the good of others in an altruistic society, which naturally brought benefit to themselves as well. Thus, by a process of change, in his case it was revolutionary not gradual change, society could progress upwards until evils like poverty, disease, vice etc., were things of the past.

Whatever we think about his theories as ideals, they failed on several fronts. First of all they did not mind which methods were employed to achieve their desired ends, since they accept that the end justifies the means. Thus in order to create a world where perfection exists, Communists will quite freely manipulate and create evil and suffering. This opposes the Christian view. Good ends can never be achieved by evil means. Jesus said that we would know people by their fruits. Evil means to secure good ends is, however, pure Evolutionary dogma where selection on a dog-eat-dog basis is necessary to produce the fittest to survive and thereby help the progression of the species.

Communists have failed just as badly in other ways because they misunderstand human nature. Christians believe that man is fallen and is by nature selfish, not altruistic. He is also sinful and therein lies the cause of humanly produced wickedness and evil.[2] To the Christian what man needs is a change of heart; a change of nature from the old wicked self to the God-given new life. Marx believed man needed a change of environment to eradicate evil and then his natural goodness would prevail. It could be said that Marx took an optimistic view of human nature and Jesus a pessimistic view but it could equally be said that Marx misjudged humanity because he eliminated God and that Jesus was not pessimistic but totally realistic.

People are not generally altruistic but are usually selfish. They seek their own good and if others benefit by their search, so be it. The truly selfless man is a rare breed (sadly even in so-called 'Christian' circles).

It is an empirical fact that men are not equal[3]. There are differences of intellect, motivation, physical capabilities, talents and nature. Some are leaders and others are followers. Man needs organisation and authority to survive. Somebody must make decisions which affect the lives of others. Whilst it would be foolish to deny that Communism has brought some benefits to the societies it seeks to serve, it would be equally foolish to deny that it has more than contributed to the load of misery its subjects suffer, many of whom discover that all they have achieved is the elimination of one form of oppression in favour of another. The socio-political way to heaven on Earth does not work.

Psychology
Modern psychological theories also attempt to cope with evil without Adam. Like Marxism they rely heavily on Evolutionary concepts to justify their arguments but are equally dependent on the deterministic viewpoint of life. Man is seen as being a product of

chemical interaction and a pure biological phenomenon. The reality of the soul or spirit is difficult to sustain, so is often reduced to 'the personality'. What to the Christian is sin, to the psychologist can be simply a chemical imbalance in the system, an unfortunate biological or sociological accident or the manifestation of unconscious forces operating on the personality from the earliest time in the womb to today. The notions of 'good' and 'evil' become relative terms and can in no way be considered as finally given or divinely stated.

Once again the psychological approach, like the socio-political approach, does have points to commend it. Many of man's irrational fears and mental disturbances can be helped by employing their techniques, but it is the *a posteriori* observation that far from being guided by irrational impulses man has the ability freely to choose and can be quite obtuse when it comes to evil. Paul analysed his own nature, saying that at times he found that 'I do not do the good I want, but the evil I do not want is what I do' (Rom. 7:19).

The Christian accepts that man has a genuine free will which he can control; the psychologist would say that in the last analysis genuine free will is illusory. If it is, then any condemnation of evil deeds is irrational either in this life or the next! We are back with the gnostics, declaring evil and suffering to be unreal!

John Hick, in his book *Death and Eternal Life* (pg. 117) demonstrates the fallacy of total determinism when he writes:

> '... any attempt rationally to establish total determinism involves the contradiction that in arguing for it the mind must presume itself not to be completely determined, but to be freely judging, recognizing logical relations, assessing relevance and considering reasons; whereas if the determinist conclusion is true the mind is, and always has been, completely determined and has never been freely judging, etc. Thus if the mind has the intellectual freedom to come to rational conclusions it cannot rationally conclude, that it is not free rationally to conclude.'

Thus whilst we recognize that there is a case for determinism frequently on a day-to-day basis, in the final analysis, when the chips really are down, we have the freedom of will freely to choose and therefore we are responsible for our decisions and actions.

Theistic Evolution
The Bible, of course, handles the problem of evil against a fully developed doctrine of the Fall. The believer who rejects a literal

Adam and, by definition therefore, a doctrine of the Fall, is left with almost insurmountable problems relating to God and His goodness. To believe that God made the world via the processes of Evolution in effect denies God's love, God's care, God's creative ability, God's rationality (one would almost say 'His sanity') and God's purposes; all of which they accept as being real.

The Theistic Evolutionist[4] would concede that God could quite easily have made the world in six literal days but that the scientific evidence proves otherwise and shows that God chose to use evolutionary mechanisms to bring His Creation into full flower. If this is true, God either allowed the world to evolve by chance or He somehow imposed His will onto the randomness of natural selection and mutations. Thus, the miracle of a six day Creation is denied but an equally impressive miracle of divinely controlled Evolution is substituted! Most Evolutionists enjoy the Darwinian theory because it eliminates the miraculous in their minds and thus turns the Theistic Evolutionist into an unwelcome bedfellow.

If God did use the evolutionary process to effect His Creation, then He did not, and still has not, perfected His work. He is still working at it! So imperfect was His original work that He unconsciously lines up with the Marxist making the end justify the means. To bring His evolving world to final perfection this evolutionary God had not only to allow evil and suffering but also to create it and sustain it positively. For Evolution to succeed, pain and suffering are vitally necessary so that the weak go to the wall. Death is an active, desirable process and not a punishment for disobedience. God, therefore, has no right, even in the feeble, imperfect scales of human justice, to blame man or a man for introducing suffering and death into the world. God claims to care for and love us, yet if Theistic Evolution is correct, He designed an evil world where man must suffer and then, as Twain rightly points out, 'tries to shuffle the responsibility for man's acts upon man, instead of honorably placing it where it belongs, upon himself.' This is pure dream, pure fantasy and does, quite seriously, throw severe doubts on God's sanity.

Apart from the fact that there is no hint of any evolutionary processes at work revealed in Scripture, Theistic Evolution is a logical nonsense. It seeks to extract the best of both worlds and in fact belongs in neither. The Evolutionist does not want God tacked onto his theories and the biblical theist will have no truck with Evolution. Evolution can explain pain but cannot help people to cope with it because it merely accepts its existence as a necessary part of life. At best, all it can produce is a stoical attitude to fate and a hopelessness in the face of the inevitable.

COPING WITH ADAM

I once heard a preacher declare that all sickness was the result of sin. He extended it to all evil and suffering. This upset my mother who had had to nurse my father and myself through years of illnesses on a major scale. If you apply a process of infinite regression to the problem of the cause of sickness, he was right, but this preacher went one stage beyond the bald statements and adopted the old Jewish idea that it was the sufferer's sins which caused his miseries. The book of Job, and later Jesus, denies that this is so, (cf John 9:1-3, Luke 13:1-5). However there is a sense in which this preacher was correct, as we have just hinted. The sin which caused sickness and death was Adam's sin when he lived in Eden (Gen 3). In Adam there is a consistent view of God (His love, Creation, control of Satan and purposes), a consistent view of evil, pain and suffering in both a human and a natural context, and a consistent theodicy. This does not mean that all questions do have an obvious answer.

If Adam was a real person, then Eden was a real state. God made the world in its full perfection; natural and human, and thus it remained until man sinned. When he sinned not only did he fall from spiritual grace and perfection, but the whole world of nature became subject to decay. As a scientist might express it, "When man fell, the Second Law of Thermodynamics began to operate." Paul indicates this truth in Romans 8:19-23:

> 'For the creation waits with eager longing for the revealing of the sons of God; for the creation was subjected to futility, not of its own will but by the will of him who subjected it in hope; because the creation itself will be set free from its bondage to decay and obtain the glorious liberty of the Children of God. We know that the whole creation has been groaning in travail together until now; and not only the creation, but we ourselves, who have the first fruits of the Spirit, groan inwardly as we wait for adoption as, sons, the redemption of our bodies.'

The doctrine of the Fall, therefore, not only deals with suffering on a human and spiritual scale but also with the world of nature. It is the only answer to the question "Why?", when applied to problems caused by earthquakes, hurricanes, flood, fire, volcanic eruptions and the like. If the world was fashioned out of violence over countless millennia, there is no such answer: and if Christians accept the scientific, rather than the biblical, world view, then they have to answer the question as to why God made a world which had in-built suffering mechanisms. It makes no sense to accept the concept of a good God who made or could have made a perfect Creation spiritually but made a most imperfect physical one. Quite rightly God's goodness and omnipotence could then be called in question. If we believe in Adam, it is quite consistent to believe that God did in fact make a perfect world which Adam's sin destroyed. This highlights the enormity of sin and it far reaching consequences. We today sometimes treat sin rather flippantly but God never does and never did. Simply eating the forbidden fruit may not rank, in our minds alongside murder, rape, adultery and theft, but it cost God His Son, subjected the world to decay and introduced sickness, pain, sorrow and death into our lives. Truly could Paul write 'As in Adam all die' (1 Cor. 15:22).

Thus belief in Adam and the Fall casts no doubt on God's creative ability. He made it every good. The world was not designed to reach perfection through suffering and death with evil as a built-in necessity, it was made perfect and technically could have thus remained. God's goodness and omnipotence are not under fire on this issue, but admittedly there are grave questions over the activities of Satan and the continuance of evil. Why does God permit evil? Why does He not eliminate it?

James writes, 'Let no-one say when he is tempted, "I am tempted by God;" for God cannot be tempted with evil and he himself tempts no-one, but each person is tempted when he is lured and enticed by his own desire. Then desire when it has conceived gives birth to sin; and sin when it is full-grown brings forth death' (Jas. 1:13-15).

Eve was enticed by her own desire and Adam followed willingly, but the Devil had a hand in it too.

Here we can present Mr. Twain with an answer and not only him but others who think like him. You remember that Twain complained about, 'a God who could make good children as easily as bad, yet preferred to make bad ones; who could have made every one of them happy, yet never made a single happy one; who made them prize their bitter life, yet stingily cut it short; who gave his angels eternal happiness unearned, yet required his other children to earn it; who gave his angels painless lives, yet cursed his other children with biting miseries and maladies of mind and body; who mouths justice and invented hell . . .'?

God did not prefer to make bad children, He made them very good. He did not 'never make a single happy one'. If we accept the implication behind Twain's attack, He made at least two very happy ones indeed. He did not give His angels eternal happiness unearned, and it was man's own fault that 'biting miseries and maladies of mind and body" came upon him. It was not Divine malice. All this is patently clear once we believe in Adam.

FREE WILL AND SATAN'S FALL

The gift of God to men and angels in Creation was free will. This gave both groups the right to use or abuse the gift. Neither had to, nor could, earn eternal happiness, for that is a gift of God. Both angels and men who use their freedom to oppose God, stand condemned and await the Judgement. Satan was one of the perfect angelic host who used his position to oppose God and thereby stands condemned just as all sinners, who have not accepted the Saviour, stand condemned.

So why does God allow evil to exist and not do anything about it? Why does he not blot out Satan and his minions? The answer is that He has done something about it! He sent Jesus to defeat the Devil and effect salvation. The problem is that God did not handle the question in the way that we would have expected. He gave and gives us His answer in Christ but it is not the answer which many want, and so God is condemned or called impotent instead of omnipotent by those who fail to recognize His gospel. The hymnwriter asked,

'And was there then no other way
For God to take? I cannot say
I only bless Him day by day
Who saved me through my Saviour.'
(from *I am not skilled to understand* by Dora Greenwell)

We question God's omnipotence without having His omniscience and that is presumptuous. It would have been a matter of contemptible ease for God to have blotted out evil and annihilated Satan but that would have meant either starting again with His Creation or going without the free gift of love which He receives from those who serve Him. He values that relationship of love so much that He tolerates an imperfect world which largely opposes Him so that He can interact in love with a few of His creatures. This says tremendous things about the love God gives and the love He wants to receive. Love is valuable to Him for He is love, and the Gospel is a message of love. To receive it carries a price — the price of pain and suffering and we can measure God's love, oddly enough, not by the happiness in the world but by looking at the evil and suffering! It is a startling truth that the creation of hell is the measure of God's love!

There is a strong body of opinion in Christendom which would suggest that a God of love could never create hell. On the contrary, a

God of love had to create hell! It is true that the Bible does say that 'God is love' but it also says that He is 'a consuming fire' and many other things as well.

Without a hell the 'love only' people are in a dilemma. They have no spiritual explanation for Christ and the Cross. Christ died to save sinners, but to save them from what? The Bible gives a clear answer, it is to save them from the wrath and justice of God; to save them from eternal condemnation. A belief in hell is necessary for a belief in the salvation Christ offers.

Fair enough; it could be pointed out that if God had not created hell in the first place then He need not have had to bother with the Cross and that this is a problem of His own making. Creating hell was the final, most complete sign of the great bounty of God. It was the stamp which said He had truly created something. Creation was a fearful and dreadful undertaking. It was not just a whim or flight of Divine fancy. The job had to be costed and part of that cost, in 'eternity past' was the Cross. Christ was 'slain before the foundation of the world'. God knew the ultimate cost of Creation but without paying that cost, God could never have created. When God gave His creatures the genuine spark of life He had to create hell. Anything less than free will for His creatures, including angelic beings, would not, as we noted in Chapter 3, have been creation but extension.

Hell was not prepared for man, it was prepared for the Devil and the angels who are his, for, on the Cross, Jesus 'slew' Satan, cast him out of heaven now to await his final condemnation. It is not God's wish that any should perish and join Satan but His love demands that He lets men choose their own destiny. We are free to follow Him or not; it is not His wish to deny any the right to choose.

Christ is the greatest expression of God's love. 'God so loved the world that he gave his only Son' (John 3:16). God without Christ, in a fallen world, is nonsense. It is hell which gives point and meaning to the life of the Saviour.

The question then remains that, if this was the price of Creation, was it worth it? Is the slightest suffering of one of God's most insignificant creatures worth this great, free Creation? God's obvious answer is 'Yes' and that says so much about heaven that words are inadequate to frame it let alone remotely come to terms with its glories. A mere human mind might well reject this but the human mind has not the depth of vision, nor the Divine insight necessary to judge. That can only happen in the future when heaven is experienced — and this is not a get-out! All humans can appreciate that probably the greatest of human experiences is the love of husband and wife in a happy marriage. They do not have to experience it before they strive for it, indeed they cannot experience it until they have it, yet its reality is never in doubt. Heaven, on a vastly different scale, has that quality.

Satan has been dealt with at Calvary. Jesus said, ' "I saw Satan fall light lightning from heaven," ' (Luke 10:18) and Revelation 12:10-11a says, 'Now the salvation and the power and the kingdom of our God and the authority of his Christ have come, for the accuser of our brethren has been thrown down, who accuses them day and night before our God. And they have conquered him by the blood of the Lamb . . .'

The Lamb shed His blood at Calvary so it was then that Satan 'fell like lightning' as a defeated foe. He is now 'in great wrath, because he knows his time is short' (Rev. 12:12). God has not annihilated Satan because God cannot annihilate any soul or spirit. They are destined for either heaven or hell; eternal bliss or eternal sorrow. The Devil awaits the Judgement before being cast into hell. (He does not live there now). God permits him to live and work on Earth just as He permits any sinner to live and work. The difference between the Devil and us is that we do have a chance to repent and be forgiven; Satan does not! Just as we are 'allowed' to commit sin and perform evil so God allows Satan the same privilege. This is called His 'permissive will'.

Not all evil is directly Satan's fault, as James said 'we are enticed by our own desire'. In a fallen world there would still be sin even if the Devil was removed. The existence of the tempter, who causes so much evil, can be thwarted if men would turn to God. Christians believe in the triumph of Christ over Satan and that God has handled him in His Divine way and is working out His purposes perfectly to the end.

CONCLUSION

I hope by now it will be clear that a belief in Adam is the only belief which can make any sense out of the problem of pain, suffering and evil. That is not say that as we see human misery in the world, as we see a battered baby or a starving child or an earthquake victim, that it is easy to say, "This is the result of sin". Innocent suffering seems so unfair and the scale of suffering such as in Nazi Germany makes one ask all sorts of "Why?" questions. Nevertheless, it *was* Adam's fault and it is the price we must pay for sin. If we have a sloppy attitude to sin, that is not God's fault. He did not, however, abandon us to our suffering but sent us the Saviour.

We are generally too easy on sin today because we have lost Adam and picked up Darwin, Freud and Marx. There is no answer to ultimate questions in any of these ungodly men. As Joshua said in a different context, " 'Choose this day whom you will serve . . . as for me and my house, we will serve the Lord" ' Josh. 24:15. You may like to follow today's 'gods' of Evolution, psychology or socio-political dogma but as for me — I believe in Adam!

NOTES

[1] The ancient Greek gods exemplified these traits.

[2] Neither Marx nor Jesus addressed themselves directly to natural disasters but a belief in Adam encompasses even these.

[3] For further discussion see Chapter 7.

[4] 'Theistic Evolutionists' are people who accept the theory of Evolution with regard to how the world and all that is in it was made but they believe it was evolution somehow controlled by God.

Chapter Five

A WORLD WITHOUT ADAM

I think it would probably be true to say that each generation believes that the world is going to the dogs and that the up-and-coming generation is the most decadent known to history. History, however, reveals that human nature remains fundamentally the same; there are good and bad in all ages, races, nations and times, and they will merely reflect the social ethos prevailing at the time. Generalisations are, however, often valid to a point and it is safe to say that, generally speaking, few people believe in Adam today. We live in a world 'without' Adam: and a world 'without' Noah and the Flood too!

Jesus said, ' "Beware of false prophets, who come to you in sheep's clothing but inwardly are ravenous wolves. You will know them by their fruits," ' (Mtt. 7:15-16). He was probably speaking solely in a religious context but today's 'faiths', which ignore God's truth as revealed in the Bible, could well be equated to wolves in sheep's clothing. They seem to offer the panacea for the world's problems and can even lull the faithful into a sense of false security, but do they bear good fruit despite their boasted claims?

ASSUMPTIONS

The biblical view of man is that he is a special, unique creation of God; that he was made perfect, fell from grace and cannot pick himself up spiritually without God's free gift of love through faith in Jesus. If he does not accept God's gift of grace, he will be forever decadent, living without purpose or goals beyond self-gratification, alienated from the true source of life which is his Creator.

The non-biblical view is that man is only a superior animal. He was never perfect so never fell but is on some sort of upward trek seeking perfection and edging ever nearer to it as time goes on. One day, given enough time, he will make it. The non-biblical view is an Evolutionary view no matter how individuals may articulate it. The theists among them would invoke the miracle or providential influence of God's help necessarily in this upward stride but the atheists would not.

These non-biblical assumptions pervaid today's thinking not only in the religious world but also in the remoter corners of life. Naturally the biological, geological and astronomical sciences rely heavily on Evolutionary thought. These sciences were largely founded on such assumptions and their current expressions would collapse like a house of cards if such foundations proved false. Reputations in academic circles would vanish and text books would need to be rewritten if Evolution was proven to be false, so there is too much pressure from vested interests in these spheres to expect a radical reappraisal of the facts overnight. Such changes can only come about gradually, as every good uniformitarian would acknowledge, like a steady drip eroding a rock!

Society as a whole seems to have adopted such concepts too. The anthropologist and archaeologist assumes that man has progressed and is progressing upwards. Indeed the very word 'progress' implies, not only a moving forwards but a moving up as well. It is possible to move forwards in a downwards direction but this is rarely acknowledged as progress. It is assumed that our ancestors were primitive in their thinking, art, science, knowledge and social environment simply because they lived thousands of years ago. It is assumed that because they are pre-historic (i.e. they left no written records) that, *a priori*, they were far inferior to us.

There must have been many very primitive people alive three or four thousand years ago, but it would be wrong to assume that all society was primitive simply because some people lived in caves for part of the year at least. If tomorrow's archaeologists based their summation of the 20th century on a careful study of the Amazonian indians or the pygmies of the Congo (Zaire) they would hardly be able to do justice to our developed Western quality of life, technology, religious thoughts, morality or social ethos. The general wood cannot adequately be described by studying one or two trees; and that is as true for studying the past as it would be for studying about today.

Civilization flourished in pre-historic and ancient times as archaeologists are only too happily aware. Indeed we seem to have lost a lot of their knowledge and to be only re-discovering things they took for granted, in our day. Civilization seems to have regressed from a glorious past into a dark age, and the steady climb out has not been continuous since man first appeared but is a much more recent phenomenon. Not only is it recent it is also patchy, confined to what we loosely call the Western world or the industrialized nations. Man is not progressing ever upwards on a global scale and the Evolutionary assumption, in a sociological context, has only a limited service to offer. All of mankind is not moving to heaven on Earth by the power invested in its own bootstraps.

There is a curious schizoid phenomenon in social evolutionary thought today. The 'isms' which most obviously reject Adam, namely Communism and Socialism, are geared to prevent social Darwinism by protecting the weak against the strong. Capitalism, which springs more directly out of the Protestant ethic based on a Calvinistic theology and claims, therefore, to be more biblically based in concept, actually also practises Darwinism in business. Marx, an avowed atheist, rejects a free society where the fittest survive and even crush the weak. He believed that the politically weak should band together to overthrow the strong, not by natural economic forces but by revolution. He did not believe in social Darwinism, though he might claim that his political system is pure Darwinism. The capitalistic societies, exemplified by the United States of America, which practise the economic survival of the fittest best, acknowledge God and are even today home to those who are leading the challenge to get back to a belief in a literal Adam and a biblical world view!. There is really no logic in a Communist/Socialist rejecting Adam and accepting a Darwinian over-view of the world and a Capitalist not being a pure Darwinian. But then consistency is not a strong human characteristic!

RESULTS

Evolutionary dogma not only pervades the scientific world it also invades almost every aspect of society where value judgements are made. If man is viewed as being merely a natural creature, just a superior animal but definitely not a special creation of God, then there is no logical reason to expect him to behave in a special way. If man is seen as having withim himself the power to rise above the moral decadence of today, then man must be the source of morality and what is right to man must be acceptable. "Do your own thing", "I did it my way" and "It's only human nature after all" are catch-phrases of such thought processes.

If man is an animal, there is no defence against such arguments. There are many things which are natural but man recognizes that he has a higher responsibility to a different moral and ethical code. Sex is natural; animals have sex, but humans make love. The ultra-permissive society which flourished in the late 1960s early 1970s enjoyed sex but many now realize that sex without love is anti-human and degrading. It leads to an unfulfilled life which is spiritually sterile. Man does not like to live at the purely animal level. An Evolutionist, theistic or not, must ask questions such as, "Why marry?", "Why not sleep around and change partners regularly?" If man is an animal, what is the virtue in being a virgin at the altar and in binding oneself in a family unit for life? Any Theistic Evolutionist has a real problem here, for he accepts God's revealed morality but rejects His revelation regarding origins. Why should God reveal a true morality and false genesis?

The permissive society makes shipwreck of lives on an individual basis, but the wider social implications of accepting a world without Adam took their most horrific form in Nazi Germany and Stalinist Russia. Hitler's 'master race' theories and Jewish genocide were the logical outcome of applied Darwinism. Here the Evolutionist is on the horns of a dilemma. He has no evolutionary basis for, what I will call for convenience, 'normal morality'. Hitler and Stalin had none, and neither does raw Communism even today, but thankfully few take the extreme line which Evolution logically demands.

The results of rejecting Adam are such that any rational being must call to question the assumptions on which the alternative view is based. If shipwrecked lives and genocide are the true results of a world without Adam, then it is about time he was re-instated!

MORALITY

There is in man, generally speaking, a sense of morality. From whence did it come? At Nuremberg (W. Germany) after the Second World War the extreme expression of Evolution which flourished under Hitler was tried and found guilty. Reference was not made to any orthodox Christian morality but to a much more nebulous, all pervading natural moral sense which was outraged at the Nazi atrocities. It was accepted that this morality existed and was a valuable reference point from which to base judgements. The Nazi war criminals merely maintained that they violated no such code, but lived and acted consistently within their ethic; they could not be tried on the basis of another ethic at all. This again is the extreme logic of the "I did it my way" and "do your own thing" kind of thinking.

Many people in society believe in what is called 'situation ethics', namely that one's morality can change to meet a situation. Thus if 'everybody's doing it', it must be acceptable. Fashions in morality come and go like fashions in the clothing industry on this basis. If homosexuality is 'in', then OK: if sex before marriage is 'in', then OK: if fiddling the tax or social security system is 'in', then OK; you can go on and on. Unfortunately for this ethic there can be no consistency or uniformity of thinking and no system of law and order can be based on it. If one man feels it is right to steal, then who is to say he is wrong? The police and courts would be totally redundant because there could be no standard to judge right and wrong; indeed the very concepts of 'right' and 'wrong' would disappear. Nobody truly believes this. The man who commits adultery is usually most upset if he is cuckolded; the thief resents being stolen from; people may want total moral freedom to do what they think is right but usually do not want such freedom to apply to others and against them. Societies which erect their own morality are frequently most severe on those who offend it.

The truth is that people do accept a moral code in broad terms. The fine detail may differ but theft, murder, rape, adultery and such actions are usually seen as violations of it. The very existence of a morality has no explanation in Darwinian terms. But, if the validity of Adam is recognized, there is no problem in discovering the source of morality. It is not derived but revealed. It comes from God. Indeed the very existence of a universally acceptable morality and a moral sense is cited as a 'proof' of the existence of God. Man, if left alone, would not produce such a sense, for man, if not a created being, could only evolve a selfish personal morality and be the sole arbiter of its validity.

CONCLUSIONS

Today we are witnessing the results of a world without Adam. The young lack direction and the old are afraid. Violence is increasing and, paradoxically, while man's technological evolution is moving ever upwards, his spiritual development is plummeting. Suicide and psychiatric sicknesses increase; people talk about depression and use drugs to lift it with far greater facility than ever before. Those who are living victoriously are those who are living as God demanded and who accept the standards He set in the Bible.

'I believe in Adam' because such a belief leads to joy and hope in a world where these commodities are ever decreasing and gives me yet another reason to ask the challenging question, "Why believe in Adam?"

Chapter Six

IF ADAM HAD NOT SINNED

Anybody who has ever remotely had a belief in Adam as a literal man must have asked themselves questions like:
— What would have happened if Adam hadn't sinned?
— Would Adam still be alive today?
— How would we feed everybody if nobody had ever died?

All such questions are highly speculative and, since the Bible does not address itself to them, all such answers must be speculative too. It could be argued that since God knew Adam would sin He saw no need to allow for the possibility that he would not sin. But, as we saw in Chapter 2, an omniscient God need not necessarily be restricted to one plan alone. When God made the world it was a world prepared for a sinless man who could have lived a sinless life but that this situation was ruined by the Fall. The doctrine of the Fall is essential to our understanding of the world God created[1] and man's accountability.

THE PHYSICAL CREATED WORLD

Before we tackle these questions head on, it is important that we grasp a few facts about the world in which God placed Adam, because it was very different from the one we know today. There are excellent books which go into a great deal of detail on this[2] and it is not my purpose to do more than summarize their conclusions.

It was the Flood of Noah's day which finally destroyed the last vestiges of the Adamic world, although the Fall began the process. In Romans 8 we read that 'the creation was subjected to futility, not of its own will but by the will of him who subjected it in hope; because the creation itself will be set free from its bondage to decay and obtain the glorious liberty of the children of God', (Rom. 8:20-21).

When Adam fell, it was not just a spiritual event but it was a cosmic event which affected the whole Universe. The perfect physical Creation became corrupted and began to decay. God had told Adam that he would die if he ate the fruit of the tree of the knowledge of good and evil but he did not die; at least not immediately. Adam died instantly spiritually (and could thereafter only be restored by grace through faith) but physical death came very much later; some 930 years later so we are told. The physical world too changed imperceptibly and thus began what we today call entropy — the Second Law of Thermodynamics — which tells us that the Universe is winding down, losing heat and moving from a state of order into a state of chaos. Scientists can measure this and find it to be true. They are not unduly worried for, if they calculate correctly and the Universe is allowed to run its full course, it will not fold-up for thousands of millions of years; but fold-up it will.

What did happen immediately after the Fall to the created world was the introduction of pain, toil and sorrow into the scheme of things. Thorns and thistles grew and we would understand that a change from vegetarianism to flesh eating occurred in the animal world (if not in the human, though it probably did even here[3]). The 'nature in the raw, tooth and claw' regime was established, and survival came to dominate the animal kingdom as well as the human world.

But what about the rest of the world? Genesis chapter 5 indicates great longevity for the antediluvian patriarchs[4]. This much-maligned chapter is only one piece of biblical evidence that the physical world before the Flood was very different from today's world. People cannot live to an average age of 912 as they did according to Genesis chapter 5 (if you exclude Enoch for he was an exception — see below). Any explanation for these great ages other than that they are true, no matter how absurd this seems to us today, falls flat on its face. Genesis 5 has a built-in consistency which betokens accurate reporting and not fictional exaggeration. Any reduction of the given ages by dividing them by factors of 8, 9 or 10, for example, creates reasonable ages for the patriarchs at death but totally absurd ages at which many of them became fathers. An examination of the ages too reveals that the Flood came 1656 years after Creation and that Methuselah died in the year of the Flood at the grand age of 969. His name apparently means, 'when he dies it comes'.

Extended longevity is quite possible if the atmopshere and climate was very different from today. The Pattens, Donald and Philip, have shown that a thicker ozone layer would reduce harmful ultra-violet radiation effects and extend life, and that an increase in the carbon dioxide content of the atmosphere would slow down maturation, causing both giantism and greater longevity[5]. They also maintain that there was a strong greenhouse effect formed by a water vapour canopy which kept temperatures uniformly high all over the globe.

There is plenty of biblical and geological evidence to support such a contention. The world of Creation was watered not by rain but by a mist (Gen. 2:6). The appearance of the rainbow as a new covenant sign (Gen 9:8-17) speaks eloquently of the fact that storms, clouds and rainfall were unknown to the antediluvian peoples. The declining longevity after the Flood shows quite clearly that there had been a major upset in the atmospheric balance which reduced man's life-span dramatically[6]. The introduction of seasons (Gen. 8:22) suggests that the Earth's axis tilted during the Flood.

Geological evidence, which Creationists would place as pre-Flood, speaks of high polar temperatures and giantism. Coal in the Antarctic and corals in the Arctic prove that at one time such areas had sub-tropical climates. Fossils from the Palaeozoic and Mesozoic eras show that many species known today had giant ancestors and, of course, the late Mesozoic saw the huge dinosaurs.

It is contended that the world which perished was a sub-tropical paradise with lush vegetation, no ice caps, no huge mountain ranges and deserts and a climate which sustained life quite comfortably[7]. There is archaeological evidence that the Sahara once bloomed[8] and that many of the world's deserts, if not actually created by man, have certainly been extended by his bad farming techniques. The Flood therefore created a landscape of mountains, valleys, deserts (hot and cold) and a world far less capable of supporting life in vast numbers than it had been before. This is consistent with a world having been created by God to sustain millions and millions of people but which man destroyed by his sin and God finally wiped out in the Flood.

IF NOBODY HAD DIED

Let us now take the questions posed at the beginning and try to answer them.

Apparently somebody has calculated that there have been approximately 74,000,000,000 people since Adam. (This may well be nearer to 75,000,000,000 today as I was given that figure quite a few years ago). Be that as it may, could the Earth support such a vast population?

The answer would be 'no' with today's uneconomical farming and scarcity of good land. There is plenty of land capable of feeding the 4,000,000,000 or so alive today with enough to spare, but it is not evenly distributed amongst the peoples or across the globe. For economic and political reasons the ground is not farmed to capacity nor is it farmed to the altruistic benefit of all. Only a world government operating totally selflessly and ruling over a populace which was not concerned with profit or personal gain could truly feed everybody, but human greed, one result of the Fall, makes this an impossible dream. However, in a sinless, perfect world where each person was concerned solely for the good of others and where the decaying, disease-ridden, rotting world we see today, did not exist, then it would be more than possible.

But would everybody still be alive and living on the Earth? Could we today go and have a chat to a very very old Adam? Let us consider the special case of Enoch.

THE 'TRANSLATION' OF ENOCH

Enoch is an enigmatic figure who appears briefly on the pages of the Bible. He was the father of Methuselah amongst others and then we read, 'Thus all the days of Enoch were three hundred and sixty-five years. Enoch walked with God; *and he was not, for God took him*' (Gen. 5:23-24, emphasis mine). All the other patriarchs listed in Genesis 5 have their paragraphs concluded with the words 'and he died'. Something else happened to Enoch. He did not die as the others did.

Hebrews 11 tells us what happened. 'By faith Enoch was taken up *so that he should not see death*, and he was not found, because God had taken him', (Heb 11:5, emphasis mine). Enoch did not die but was translated smoothly from this earthly life into the heavenly life without dying. There was no pain or sorrow, just a lovely smooth movement from one existence into another. I believe that here we glimpse what God intended for us all if we had not sinned.

We would not have tasted death but we would have been smoothly translated into heaven once our time came. It would have been a joyous event; one to be anticipated eagerly. Our families would be glad and rejoice and we would not even know the word 'death' at all.

Thus Adam would not still have been here on Earth he would long since have been translated. The Earth would not have had to support 74 or 75 thousand million people no matter how efficiently it was farmed.

BE FRUITFUL AND MULTIPLY

The above conclusion is reinforced by the command which Adam and Eve were given in Genesis 1. 'And God blessed them, and God said to them, "Be fruitful and multiply, and fill the earth and subdue it," ' (Gen. 1:28). If God had intended man to live eternally on Earth in his sinless state, there would have come a point where man could not sustain life from the Earth's resources so God would have had to have stopped the reproductive function and rescind this command. It would also mean that God never wanted man in heaven with Him, yet heaven (which is purely a spiritual state) is our real home and destiny, living forever in sinless perfection. Whilst here on Earth, Adam may not have sinned but sin was always a possibility and somebody else no doubt would have done so, sooner or later.

To leave Adam here would not have been to leave him living in the perfect state because his physical nature would not have been cast aside. Heaven always was our home and Earth our hotel.

Thus I believe we do receive a window into the original eternal plan for the world in the first elevan chapters of Genesis. Whether I am correct or not, one thing shines through and that is the great sinfulness of sin and just what Eve did when she picked and ate the fruit and gave it to Adam.

NOTES

[1] See Chapter 3 'The World Which God Created'.

[2] See Bibliography.

[3] Genesis 9 v3 is the point at which meat eating became official but it is quite probable that man indulged beforehand.

[4] See my book *Speak Through the Earthquake, Wind and Fire, op cit*, pages 54-56.

[5] *Ibid*.

[6] See D.W. Patten's book *The Biblical Flood and the Ice Epoch*, pub. Pacific Meridan Publishing Co. Seattle, USA (1966).

[7] *Ibid*.

[8] *Encyclopoedia Britannica*, 15th Edition (1977), Macropaedia, Vol 16, pages 148-150.

Chapter Seven

THE ROLE OF THE SEXES

The only truly successful way to live in a relationship involving the sexes is to live as God tells us in the Bible. This may be provocative and many feminists would be totally up in arms at the thought because they frequently seem to misunderstand the biblical picture. If husbands had treated their wives biblically down the years, we would never have heard of Feminism, Women's Lib., Suffragettes and the like; and if wives had tried to live as God directed them, their husbands would never have given them cause to see their men as 'male chauvinist pigs'. God's beautiful balance which glories in individual sexuality as equal but different, brings bliss when followed and misery when denied. Men and women are not the same; and it goes much deeper than mere physical sexuality, it goes into their basic psyche and runs through the whole gamut of their emotional, spiritual and intellectual experiences. The sexes complement each other in perfect harmony when men recognize their rôle and fulfil it and women do likewise. It is never a case of superiority versus inferiority but a blend of equals working differently but together.

It is sad today to see women fighting for their rights, real or imaginary. In their strident attempts to win social equality, many have come to deny their femininity and seem almost to resent being women. Being a women is a wonderful thing which brings blessings men can never begin to comprehend. The reverse is also true and it is crazy to see unisex as an idea propounded in society. Sexual Equality Acts and Sex Discrimination Acts are a travesty. One of the saddest pieces of legislation enacted in Britain was when the tax exemption fôr children was taken off the man's wages and added to the child benefit allowance which is made out to the mothers. It was a sad comment on the selfishness and lack of working together which characterizes many marriages. Paul wrote, 'Husbands love your wives as your own bodies' (Eph. 5:28), and if they obeyed that simple command this situation could not occur.

The foundation for all sexual relationships is laid in Genesis 1-11, so let us examine the issues which are raised there.

CAIN'S WIFE

First of all we must clear away the old 'chestnut' of 'where did Cain get his wife?' before we tackle some real problems.

Proponents of evolutionary theories frequently challenge Creationists with this question because Cain seemed to have had a wife and family when he murdered Abel and no daughters of Adam are mentioned in the Bible up to that point. And again, if Cain's wife was his sister, then God must have encouraged incest which He later condemned as wrong. Consequently, they reason that Cain's wife must have come from the pool of humanoids which evolved simultaneously with Adam.

Those who are Theistic Evolutionists maintain that Genesis 1:26-28 describes the creation, not of a single man, but of many. Adam means 'man' or 'mankind' and God put many men and women on Earth at once, by Evolution of course. They see Genesis 2 as a concentration on one family, if it has any reality which they usually deny, so Cain got his wife from one of the other families around at the time. Atheistic Evolutionists deny Adam in any form and thus have no problem here.

There need be no problem at all for anybody. In Genesis 1:28 God said, ' "Be fruitful and multiply; and fill the earth and subdue it." ' Just because Genesis 4 concentrates on the story of two of their children and does not deal with the rest of their family, it does not mean that they had only produced two lads up to this point. Indeed Genesis 5:4 tells us that Adam 'had other sons and daughters'; a whole tribe of them. There is no reason to doubt Cain's wife was his sister.

But then doesn't God forbid incest? Yes, He does, specifically in the Law of Moses (Lev. 18:6-18 for example), but He did not reveal His complete will on every matter all at once. The biblical record is one of progressive revelation until 'the faith (was) once for all delivered to the saints' (Jude 3). Abraham's wife Sarah was his half-sister, the daughter of his father to a different mother (Gen. 20:12), and this marriage too would have been considered incestuous according to the levitical law. God prohibits incest because of the grave biological probability of congenital idiots being born to such relationships, as much as for moral reasons. When He gives a moral law, it always makes good physical and psychological sense even to an unbelieving world. He had to allow it to get the world going but it would not have been in man's best interests to allow it to continue for too long, so He banned it. This is not inconsistency, but common sense; God has never been short of that!

MARRIAGE

Christians have always maintained that full sexual relations are beautiful, full of meaning and purpose and are a blessing from God but they must occur only within the context of marriage and with the one partner.

Adultery and fornication are roundly condemned in the Bible. It is a sad comment but true, a young Christian once admitted that she always knew adultery was wrong but nobody had ever told her, before she became a Christian, what fornication meant. Whilst she had lived in the world she had followed the world when many were saying that adultery is wrong because it breaks up marriages but sex before marriage or fornication, is fine; it can even be beneficial because it helps couples see if they are sexually compatible. This too is a fallacy and frequently puts strains on relationships later when people marry.

When Jesus wanted to teach about marriage He went right back to Genesis. There in Chapter 2 we read, 'Therefore a man leaves his father and his mother and cleaves to his wife, and they become one flesh,' (v. 24). When questioned about divorce Jesus said, ' "Have you not read that he who made them from the beginning made them male and female, and said, 'For this reason a man shall leave his father and mother and be joined to his wife and the two shall become one flesh?' So they are no longer two but one flesh," ' (Mtt. 19:5-6). Here is the teaching that God intended two to become one. He never wanted polygamy, though He acquiesced in the Old Testament.[1]

Two becoming one is the basis for marriage and Jesus went back to Adam to show it. When two strive to remain as two yet adopt a married rôle they cause trouble for themselves. Marriage is selfless love where each one seeks the perfect good of the other. It is a window into heaven and the relationship of love which God wants with us. The lover seeks only the good of the beloved and thereby receives pure, spiritual happiness. It is when one or both is selfish that trouble starts.

It has been said that God took woman out of man's side so she could stand equally alongside him. She did not come from his head to rule over him nor from his feet to serve him but from his side to support him. This was always God's intention. Woman is neither inferior nor superior to man in Creation but was made to be a helpmeet. It is impossible to understand the God-intended rôle if Genesis 1-11 is relegated to the status of myth or legend. The authority of Jesus, who accepted Adam as a fact, should be enough to clinch it but sadly it is not, even for many people who call themselves Christians.

It is true to say that men have misused women down the millennia since Creation. They see in the Fall and the curse on Eve a God-given right to rule over women, whereas it was simply clarifying the God-intended rôle of the sexes in the new situation when God said, ' "I will greatly multiply your pain in childbearing; in pain you shall bring forth children, yet your desire shall be for your husband, and he shall rule over you," ' (Gen. 3:16). The curse was that women will have pain in childbirth NOT that their husband will rule them. God was saying, "You will have great pain, nevertheless you will still want children ('your desire will be for your husband')". He added that the man will be head of the house and that this is the situation in which women will find most comfort and happiness. When a man takes on his rôle as head of the house he gives his woman the love and security she needs to be happy and raise their children in a loving stable family. When a man denies his rôle or a woman refuses to let him adopt it, there is trouble with the caricature marriage of the domineering wife beloved of cartoonists and satirists.

Paul amplifies the relationship best in Ephesians 5:21-33. Here he links the married state to that of Christ and the church and shows it to be not only an earthly relationship but also a heavenly one. We shall return to this a little later but for now let us simply detail the instructions aimed specifically at husbands and wives:

> 'Be subject to one another out of reverence for Christ. Wives be subject to your husbands, as to the Lord. For the husband is the head of the wife, so let wives also be subject in everything to their husbands. Husbands love your wives, husbands should love their wives as their own bodies. He who loves his wife loves himself. For no man ever hates his own flesh, but nourishes and cherishes it . . . Let each one of you love his wife as himself, and let the wife see that she respects her husband.'

This is the formula for a successful marriage.

The passage begins with a statement of equality — 'Be subject to one another.' It is not the rôle of either partner to lord it over the other. In 1 Corinthians 7:4, Paul wrote 'For the wife does not rule over her own body, but the husband does; likewise the husband does not rule over his own body but the wife does.'

How dare people say that Paul is a male chauvinist; he was one of the original female liberators! He gave women equal dignity with men in a world which had long forgotten God's creative plan. Where he differed from today's liberators is that he recognized the eternal teachings of God, that the sexes are different and therefore have a different function to play in marriage, and incidentally in the church. He knew that in Christ 'there is neither male nor female' (Gal. 3:28), but this referred to their standing before God and not to their earthly, human rôles.

Then he proceeds to detail the attitudes each partner should adopt towards the other. He gives his reasons which are that eternal priniciples are figured in a marriage and this shows that these rules are not his own biases, as many liberal scholars contend.

Any man, who reads Paul's words to wives and rubs his hands with glee, is very soon cut down to size. No man could possibly boss his wife, treat her like a slave, ignore her desires and pleasures, disregard her opinions or treat her as anything other than a beloved equal once he reads that he must love his wife as he loves himself. No man would like to be treated either in action or attitude as many men have treated their womenfolk; thus if Paul's teaching was followed, all marriages would be blissfully happy. He was only echoing Jesus' words in Matthew 7:12, ' "Whatever you wish that men would do to you, do so to them," ' but, like Jesus, he too went right back to Genesis 2:24 for his authority in his instructions (Eph. 5:31).

The basis then for successful marriage is found in Genesis 2. Paul and Jesus both cite it as authority for their teaching and, as we all desire to live happily in our marriages, the Genesis record must not be disregarded. Relegate it to the level of myth, legend, or saga and the foundation of Christian teaching in this area is not even built on sand — let alone solid rock. I want a happy marriage, so I believe in Adam.

DIVORCE

The Bible, as we have noted, is quite clear about the rôle of the sexes in marriage. If adhered to, there would be no divorce because there could be no bad marriages. Many divorces start with unbiblical choices of mate. Christians are told not to be 'mismated with unbelievers' (2 Cor. 6:14) but to marry 'in the Lord' (1 Cor. 7:39). Mixed 'religious' marriages rarely result in spiritual triumph. What usually happens is that the non-Christian weans the Christian away from the faith.[2]

But we are all human and do not always make wise, biblical choices. Sometimes this can lead to intolerable situations and we feel like getting a divorce; so what does the Bible have to say about that?

The Bible takes a very serious view of marriage and divorce. Politicians may make and change the law of the land to suit the prevailing social climate but God is not so fickle. The first thing to remember is that every married person is under a vow and vows in God's eyes are very serious things. It is no use complaining that "we had our fingers crossed when we made our vows" and feel we can get out that way. In Numbers we read, 'When a man vows a vow to the Lord, or swears an oath to bind himself by a pledge, he shall not break his word: he shall do according to all that proceeds out of his mouth' (Num. 30:2). The marriage vow is an oath and we must keep it whether it turns nasty or not. The great judge Jephthah made a rash vow and was forced to sacrifice his only child, a beloved daughter, as a result (Judges 11); but he is listed in the famous list of the faithful (Heb. 11:32) because he kept his vow to God even when it rebounded horribly on himself.

At our marriage we make a solemn vow to love and cherish the beloved, for richer or poorer, in sickness and in health, for better *or worse*. If it turns out worse than we took it for, we are still under a vow and vows are sacred.

What then does the Bible teach about divorce? Let us turn to what many feel is the definitive passage in Matthew 19 and see what Jesus said.

> 'And Pharisees came up to him and tested him by asking, "Is it lawful to divorce one's wife for any cause?" He answered, "Have you not read that he who made them from the beginning made them male and female, and said, "For this reason a man shall leave his father and mother and be joined to his wife, and the two shall become one flesh?" So they are no longer two but one flesh. What therefore God has joined together, let not man put assunder." They said to him, "Why then did Moses command one to give a certificate of divorce, and to put her away?" He said to them, "For your hardness of heart Moses allowed you to divorce your wives, but from the beginning it was not so. And I say to you: whoever divorces his wife, except for unchastity, and marries another, commits adultery," (Mtt. 19:3-9).

Earlier in Matthew's gospel we read of Jesus saying, in the Sermon on the Mount, ' "It was also said, 'Whoever divorces his wife, let him give her a certificate of divorce.' But I say to you that every one who divorces his wife, except on the ground of unchastity, makes her an adulteress; and whoever marries a divorced woman commits adultery," ' (Mtt. 5:31-32).

Here then is an unequivocal statement of the Divine teaching on divorce and it goes right back to Adam. Jesus showed that two become one and it was never God's intention to allow divorce. Indeed in Malachi 2:15-16 (speaking admittedly of God's relationship to Israel) we read, 'So take heed to yourselves, and let none be faithless to the wife of his youth. For I hate divorce, says the Lord the God of Israel'.

Reading such words on marriage and divorce it is easy to see God's original intentions. It was to be one man to one woman with no polygamy and no divorce, except for adultery. When Moses came and taught the Jews about divorce, he was not liberalizing God's strictures he was tightening up man's laxity. In the pre-Exodus world divorce apparently was easy, if you were a man! Moses merely regularized it and gave women some rights where before they had had none (Deut. 24:1-4).

There was actually no need to give an 'exception clause' under the old Law. Jesus said that adultery, (unchastity), is the sole reason for divorce but under the mosaical law an adulterer or adulteress should have been stoned! If the law was strictly adhered to, the innocent party would then be widowed and therefore free to re-marry in the normal way.

Reading what Jesus said in Matthew we can see clearly the one reason for divorce which is allowed under Christian law: adultery. Why should this be? When two people are joined together they become one flesh. Any man or any woman who commits adultery joins their bodies to the body of another and becomes one with their adulterous partner. They break the unity of the flesh with their married partner and thus the exclusiveness which binds them together is severed, so divorce is then allowed.

Jesus, however, taught a greater law namely that of forgiveness. He did not say that the adulterer *must* be divorced but that he or she can be. His way was not to condemn but to forgive. When the Jews chased foreign gods it was seen as an adultery on their part but God, like Hosea, took them back. He used Hosea to illustrate his loving forgiveness even though Israel played the harlot. The Christian must always first seek the path of forgiveness rather than divorce.

No doubt this raises as many questions as it solves. People will ask about batterings, desertions, intolerable behaviour etc.. The answer comes back that you must be reconciled. If you cannot live together, there is nothing against separation but those separated must live as single people and not fornicate or commit adultery, (1 Cor. 7:10-11).

The church at Corinth faced a situation which we still find today. All the above, of course, about divorce is applied solely to Christians. The question then is posed, "What if one of the partners in a non-Christian marriage becomes a Christian and faces problems?"

Paul addressed himself to this in 1 Cor. 7. Here he wrote,

> 'To the married I give charge, not I but the Lord, that the wife should not separate from her husband (but if she does, let her remain single or else be reconciled to her husband) — and that the husband should not divorce his wife.
>
> 'To the rest, I say, not the Lord, that if a brother has a wife who is an unbeliever, and she consents to live with him, he should not divorce her. If any woman has a husband who is an unbeliever, and he consents to live with her, she should not divorce him....
>
> 'But if the unbelieving partner desires to separate, let it be so: in such a case the brother or sister is not bound,' (1 Cor. 7:10-15).

We note here that marriage is sacred even if the couple were not Christians when they were married. If one partner becomes a Christian, the mariage is sanctified and the commitment is still binding. There is no get-out clause by claiming that a pagan or secular ceremony is invalid. There is no ceremony described in Scripture and what is considered binding on earth is bound in heaven.

We note too that separation is allowable but, as mentioned above, the separated ones must recognize that they are not free and must live as single, chaste believers or be reconciled.

Now it is fair to say that this question of divorce is a difficult one and that there are many ramifications. It is not the purpose of this chapter to go into all of them and finish up with the definitive answer to all possible questions. That would really require a separate book. People ask, "What if a couple were divorced and re-married before they became Christians? Should they consider their second marriage as adulterous and stop living together, or sleeping together? Can the innocent party in an adulterine divorce re-marry? Can the guilty party re-marry?" There are some groups who believe that Matthew was writing for Jews and the 'adultery' clauses refer to adultery after betrothal but before marriage, such as Joseph suspected Mary of committing. These groups will not allow divorce at all.

In some instances it is easy to reply, in others not. The innocent party to an adulterine divorce is obviously free to re-marry since it was his or her partner's adultery which severed the vow. But can the other re-marry? This is hotly debated and we enter the realm of opinion — my opinion — which is not inspired.

I believe that the adultery clause was not referring to the Jewish betrothal period only, but is valid for all Christians. Those who believe differently must establish that Matthew was written specifically for Jews *and* that this referred to that period only. They also have the onus of explaining why the adulterous one was not to be stoned. Jesus did not legislate for Judaism; His teaching is for Christians.

I believe that a couple who were married prior to becoming Christians and one or both were divorced and that their marriage, if made as believers would be considered adulterous, cannot be so considered. They were not bound by God's laws. They need not worry. Just as our other sins are buried in baptism, so this one too is forgiven.

I believe that the adulterous partner, the guilty party, cannot re-marry if he was a Christian and still seeks to remain one. (He can do as he pleases, no doubt, if he becomes apostate).

Can a divorcee be married in church? This too, is hotly debated. *I believe* if he or she is the innocent party in an adulterine divorce, the answer is 'Yes'. In other cases as Christians, they cannot re-marry anyway. Could pre-Christian divorcees re-marry as Christians? I believe they can.

Notice in all the above '*I believe*' is emphasized because there is no direct teaching in the Bible. You may believe something else, and so might I in my later years. This is my *opinion* and my opinion only at the time of writing, and I am not inspired.

The point about this section on divorce, and the previous one on marriage, is that where we have clear teaching we go back to Adam. If we jettison our belief in Adam, as a literal man, we have no grounds for maintaining that God's original intention was monogamy and that divorce, 'save for unchastity', is not allowable to those who want to call themselves Christians. Jesus took His teaching right back to Adam, and so must we.

IN THE CHURCH

Another hotly debated topic today is the rôle of the sexes within the church. Many feel that women should be given equal facilities to lead worship, pray, read, celebrate communion, preach etc.. Any public office currently given solely to men should be opened to women — so they say. It is here that they quote Paul to prove their point and then later condemn him as a male chauvinist. How could the man who could write that 'there is neither male or female ...in Christ Jesus' (Gal. 3:28) also write, 'Let a woman learn in silence with all submissiveness. I permit no woman to teach or have authority over men; she is to keep silent,' (1 Tim. 2:11-12) and similar words in 1 Cor. 14:33-36? Is he being inconsistent?

The answer, of course, is 'no'. Paul would see no inconsistency in his writings, nor is there any. Galatians is not dealing with practicalities of worship in the churches but with eternal matters. In his day the Jews, and society in general, felt that certain categories of people were inferior to others. The Jews felt that Gentiles (Greeks), slaves and females were vastly inferior to free, male Jews. In Christ there is no distinction. In Christianity nobody is superior or inferior but that does not mean that there are not different functions in the church, which are not always open to all.

Paul, in fact, details this principle in his first Corinthian letter. His famous passage on the body being composed of many parts, each one vital to the harmony of the whole and with no part inferior in God's eyes (1 Cor. 12:12-29), illustrates the point. We are all equal but we do not all have the same function. This applies equally to men and women as well as to elders and deacons.

We have noted this principal earlier when we considered the rôle of the sexes in marriage. Just as men and women are equal but have different rôles within that relationship, so too in the church. Indeed, marriage is the type which figures the eternal relationship which Jesus has with His bride — the church. Paul drew this analogy in the Ephesians 5 passage we considered earlier. Let a quotation from the middle of his argument suffice to make the connection:

> 'Husbands should love their wives as their own bodies. He who loves his wife loves himself. For no man ever hates his own flesh but nourishes and cherishes it, as Christ does the church, because we are members of his body. 'For this reason a man shall leave his father and mother and be joined to his wife, and the two shall become one flesh.' This mystery is a profound one, and I am saying that it refers to Christ and the Church; however, let each one of you love his wife as himself, and let the wife see that she respects her husband.' (Eph. 5:28-33).

The rôle of the sexes in marriage and in the church should reflect the eternal relationship between Christ and the church. This is an absolutely consistent theme in the New Testament.

When dealing with the Corinthians, Paul had to correct them because they had not grasped this fact. Their new found equality and freedom in Christ was being taken beyond that eternal relationship and the women were forgetting themselves (and the men were letting them!). The early part of Chapter 11 deals with veiling women in the assembly (verses 2-16) and so eternal relationships are pointed out:

> 'But I want you to understand that the head of every man is Christ, the head of a woman is her husband and the head of Christ is God.... For a man ought not to cover his head since he is the image and glory of God; but woman is the glory of man. (For man was not made from woman, but woman from man. Neither was man created for woman, but woman for man)... (Nevertheless, in the Lord woman is not independent of man nor man of woman; for as woman was made from man, so man is now born of woman. And all things are from God).'

Here is the now familiar reasoning again and it goes right back to Adam for its verification. Much of Paul's theology (and Christology — see Chapter 10) depends on the reality of Adam.

So within the church the eternal relationship must be reflected in its organisation and worship. The unique rôles of the males must not be usurped by the females. It may not suit many of today's feminists to accept this but, just as it works beautifully when lovingly applied in marriage and is the correct formula for marital happiness and earthly bliss, so it is correct for spiritual happiness and heavenly bliss. All of us are subject to somebody or something — even Christ subjected Himself to the Father. The trouble with many today is that they want to be subject to nobody but themselves and feel such subjection is a denial of their personality in some way.

Thus in a congregation of the saints it is men who pray publicly, preach, teach, lead the meetings and take the fronting rôles. This in no way makes them superior to those whose rôle is in background service. The ear must not say 'Because I am not an eye, I do not belong to the body' (1 Cor. 12:16). Not all men are given the talent or calling to lead in public worship and no matter how painful it may be to a woman to be denied these rôles, she must show her subjection (i.e. her correct relationship to God and her husband) by not seeking to usurp his function. If she does, she becomes the ecclesiastical equivalent of the cartoon, domineering, unfeminine woman.

CONCLUSION

I know much of what is written in this chapter will upset some people because it will seem to put the 'cause of women', whatever that may be, back several centuries. The happiest people are those who live as God directed. Strident feminists never seem to me to be fulfilled. How can they be when they seek to deny their sexuality and want to behave like men?

God gave the sexes different rôles and only in the outworking of these rôles does true happiness exist. At all points in the biblical argument the base point is the edenic situation of earthly paradise and the events found in Genesis 1 — 11.

That is yet another reason why I believe in Adam.

NOTES

[1] Solomon had 700 wives and 300 concubines! (1 Kings 11:3).

[2] I am not here addressing the situation where two non-Christians marry and one is later converted. That provides a totally different set of circumstances.

Chapter Eight

JUDGEMENT AND HELL

We all have our own ideas about heaven. Some may feel that it has no reality at all and is merely a nice idea but surveys have shown that a majority believe in heaven and not only want to go there but also believe that they will! Hell does not fare quite so well. It is a peculiar person who wants to go there although I did meet a rather sad teenager once who said he wanted to go to hell. ' "Hell's where all the action is," he exclaimed vehemently. "All the women you want, all the booze you want, all the good times you want are in Hell. Heaven's boring; who wants to go there?" ' The same surveys, which reveal a heaven-bound belief in the majority, reveal a hell-denying certainty amongst the same group. There is more misguided rationalizing of hell, or more simply head-burying in the sand over hell, than over any other single biblical topic.

The plain truth is that for many their ideas of God are erroneous. We have noted earlier how a wrong concept of God affects all our thinking and it does equally at this point too. We have probably all heard the statement that a God of love could not condemn any to eternal punishment. Some will quite happily accept the idea of a spell of torment for sinners with graded sentences depending on how bad they were on Earth. Thus a Hitler or a Nero will have a very long spell in the flames until they have purged their sins; but not hell for ever! Not everlasting, eternal, unending, total condemnation for big and little sinners alike. A God of love could never do that — it is argued.

It can be argued for as long as people choose but the picture which emerges from the Bible is that hell, whatever it is, is for ever; and the roots of the doctrine of punishment and judgement lie in Genesis 1-11.

SALVATION FROM WHAT?

The Bible teaches the need to be saved and that this need is urgent, for once we die we face judgement (Heb. 9:27). Salvation is so important that God sent His only Son into the world to die so that those who truly believe in Him will be saved.

Why did Jesus come to Earth? Why was He prepared, 'though he was in the form of God, not to count equality with God a thing to be grasped, but to empty himself and take the form of a servant being born in the likeness of men; and, being found in human form, to humble himself and become obedient unto death, even death on a cross'? (Phil. 2:6-8). If there was no reality to hell at all, or if it was to be only for a period of time until our sins were purged, there would have been no need for, nor any logic in, His coming! God could merely have allowed us to live; tot up our sins when we die; pronounce a certain period of purging until we had paid for our misdeeds; and then welcome us all back into heaven.

There is no logic in the story of the incarnation and the cross if eternal hell is not a reality.

BACK TO THE FALL

Gospel preachers proclaim that Jesus conquered death in His resurrection; rising victorious over the tomb. The Bible teaches that once we were perfect but when sin entered the world so did death (Rom. 5:12). Death was to be the punishment for eating the forbidden fruit (Gen. 2:16-17). The death which Jesus arose victorious over was not simply physical death — it was spiritual death. Jesus warned us, ' "do not fear those who kill the body and after that have no more that they can do. But I will warn you whom to fear; fear him who, after he has killed, has power to cast into hell; yes, I tell you, fear him!" ' (Luke 12:4-5).

All Christians believe that they have everlasting life but not in this physical realm. We will all die a physical death, Jesus did not prevent that, but we will not all die the second or spiritual death.

Adam did not immediately die physically when he sinned but he died instantly spiritually. Nevertheless his physical death became inevitable once he sinned.

Now, if Adam evolved, death was not a punishment but the natural process of life by which God brought man into being. Adam, whoever he was, would not have seen in death, physical death, any figure or warning about his spiritual state. The introduction of physical death showed the reality of spiritual death too. Christ's victory would have been shallow and without substance if God was going to save everybody ultimately anyway.

We need a doctrine of the Fall to make any sense of Jesus and the incarnation; but we will return to this in our final chapter. Jesus died because man fell from grace when he sinned; Jesus died because, without His shed blood, we would all spend eternity in an existence where God is not and this is a terrifying state in which to be.

HELL

You may well have seen a cartoon which shows a poster outside a church building with words something like this, 'What hell is like. Come and hear our speaker, Mr. Farley, on Sunday at 6.30 p.m.' Hell, whatever it may be is not a bad sermon — agonizing though that can be!

To many minds the concept of Gehenna, where fire burns endlessly, is crude and inefficient. The mataphor is drawn from the Hinnom valley where the fires of the Jerusalem rubbish tips ceaselessly burned human effluent in Jesus' day. Spiritual dross will likewise be consumed. The 'lake of fire' concept from Revelation could also be drawn from volcanic phenomena. If we believe hell is 'down there', then looking into a volcano is like looking into the under-world. It is a terrifying picture vividly conjuring up an image of sulphur, heat and pain.

But far more terrifying than this is the picture of a place where God is not. All the blessings which God showers on saint and sinner alike whilst they are alive, will not be present in hell. In Galatians there is a lovely list of the fruit of the Spirit. When we realize that in hell none of these will exist then we catch a glimpse perhaps of its awesome reality. In hell there will be no love, joy, peace, patience, kindness, goodness, faithfulness, gentleness, self-control' (Gal. 5:22-23). Pondering an existence like that is far more spine-chilling than any lake of fire. My pupil, who had an erroneous picture of heaven and declared it to be boring, got it all wrong. It is hell which will be boring. Boredom is not a 'gift' of God, so will be completely absent from heaven but present in its fulness in hell.

Christians know that in Jesus we see the love of God in its beauty and He above all taught us about God's love. Yet the irony of the situation is this — that He who was total love whilst on Earth taught most about the eternal reality of hell. God may be love but that is not all He is. He is also righteous, holy and just, a consuming fire. Whilst because of His love 'He gave His only Son as a sacrifice for sins,' nevertheless the holy, righteous justice of His nature demands retribution on all who reject His Son, spurn His love, and deny His grace. His patience means that He gives more and more time for men to repent, and He gives each sinner countless opportunities to repent, but one day He will close down on sin forever. There will be no escape for all who are outside of Christ; rather, a fierce and terrible judgement.

RESURRECTION

The picture Jesus paints is consistent with this belief. In John's gospel we read about the resurrection of two categories of people, the good and the evil, who both rise on the last day and are judged and sentenced. The good will receive life and the evil will receive judgement.

> ' "Truly, truly, I say to you, the hour is coming, and now is, when the dead will hear the voice of the Son of God, and those who hear will live. For as the Father has life in himself, so he has granted the Son also to have life in himself, and has given him authority to execute judgement, because he is the Son of man. Do not marvel at this; for the hour is coming when all who are in the tombs will hear his voice and come forth, those who have done good, to the resurrection of life, and those who have done evil, to the resurrection of judgement," ' (John 5:25-29).

For those who think that the good will go to heaven and the evil will be annihilated, this passage clearly denies the idea of an annihilation. It also denies the idea that at Christ's second appearance only the saved will rise, leaving the evil below. All souls, irrespective of their final destination, will rise.

Jesus warned the Jews that ' "the sons of the kingdom will be thrown into outer darkness, there men will weep and gnash their teeth," ' (Mtt. 8:12). In the parable of the wheat and tares He spoke of fire, weeping and gnashing of teeth; of judgement and reward.

> ' "Just as the weeds are gathered and burned with fire, so will it be at the close of the age. The Son of man will send his angels, and they will gather out of his kingdom all causes of sin and all evildoers, and throw them into the furnace of fire; there men will weep and gnash their teeth. Then the righteous will shine like the sun in the kingdom of their Father," ' (Mtt. 13:40-43).

Finally, in the famous judgement scene passage of Mtt. 25:31-45, Jesus concludes that the wicked ' "will go away into eternal punishment, but the righteous into eternal life." ' Note that it is to be *eternal.*

Not only is it to be eternal but it is to be consciously eternal. That may sound strange or self-evident but the picture Jesus painted of life after death is of conscious existence where each one of us has a recognizable identity. In the story of Lazarus and the Rich Man as told by Luke (chapter 16:19-31), Jesus talks of Abraham as a conscious personality as well as of Lazarus and the Rich Man. There was a conversation across the great gulf as the Rich Man begged that Lazarus be allowed to dip his finger in water so that his tongue, which was in fiery agony, could be cooled.

The idea of conscious existence after death is consistent with the transfiguration of Jesus where He talks with Moses and Elijah, with the witch of Endor (1 Sam. 28:1-19) where Samuel comes back, and with resurrection passages such as 1 Corinthians 15. We will be recognizable in the spirit world; have a celestial body and will consciously communicate with others. It will not be a great mixing with the life force; we will have a conscious personality. However, we will not experience human-like relationships. There will be no sexual activity, for instance, but we will be like the angels (Luke 20:34-36).

Hell, no matter how we conceptualize it, will be eternal, conscious punishment. A state definitely to be avoided.

JUDGEMENT

You cannot have a heaven or a hell without a judgement. Heaven and hell are the end products of God's judgement on mankind. Genesis 1-11 may not speak directly of hell but it speaks most eloquently of the end of Divine patience and the wrath of God's justice.

The same Jesus who spoke so forcefully of hell spoke equally forcefully of a judgement. He went straight back to Noah and the Flood for His proof that judgement will come:—

' "As were the days of Noah, so will be the coming of the Son of man. For as in those days before the flood they were eating and drinking, marrying and giving in marriage until the day when Noah entered the ark, and they did not know until the flood came and swept them all away, so will be the coming of the Son of man," ' (Mtt. 24:37-40).

He then goes on to tell parables of how we should all be alert and watch and not bury our talents or we will be cast out. Then He gives His graphic picture of the judgement where all nations are gathered before His throne and divided into sheep and goats. The sheep, who did His will, are sent to eternal life and the goats, who did not do His will, are sent to eternal punishment (Mtt. 25:31-46).

The reality of the Flood may not be accepted by modern liberal scholars; it is also denied by orthodox geologists but there is plenty of evidence, extant today, which suggests that it is these people who are astray. It is not my brief to deal with this evidence in this book but volumes like *The Genesis Flood* by Whitcomb and Morris tackle it head on.

The apostle Peter predicted that men would deny the coming of the Lord in judgement by forgetting or ignoring the reality of the Flood. In a most profound passage he writes,

'First of all you must understand this, that scoffers will come in the last days with scoffing following their own passions and saying, "Where is the promise of his coming? Forever since the fathers fell asleep, all things have continued as they were from the beginning of creation. They deliberately ignore this fact, that by the word of God heavens existed long ago, and an earth formed out of water and by means of water, through which the world that then existed was deluged with water and perished. But by the same word the heavens and earth that now exist have been stored up for fire, being kept until the day of judgement and destruction of ungodly men.' (2 Pt. 3:3-7).

The reality of the day of judgement is clearly linked to the reality of the Flood, for both Jesus and Peter. Jesus does not query the doubt of disbelievers but uses Noah's day to illustrate, quite naturally, what it will be like before He appears in judgement. It will be monotonously uneventful. The only warnings given to a faithless world will be via the faithful preaching of godly men. He will come 'like a thief in the night', quite unexpectedly. The wise will be ready (Mtt. 25:9) but the foolish will be caught out (Mtt. 25:12-13).

Peter tells us that the world of this day will be consumed with fire. Paul tells us that,

'God deems it just to reply with affliction those who afflict you, and to grant rest with us who are afflicted, when the Lord Jesus is revealed from heaven with his mighty angels in flaming fire, inflicting vengeance upon those who do not know God and upon those who do not obey the gospel of our Lord Jesus. They shall suffer the punishment of eternal destruction and exclusion from the presence of the Lord and from the glory of his might, when he comes on that day to be glorified in his saints, and to be marvelled at in all who have believed,' (2 Thess. 1:6-10).

A denial of the first destruction of the world and the judgement on that generation, is a denial of the reality of any judgement. Yet it is one of the strongest of all biblical truths. The saved, like Noah, will be preserved in God's loving arms, but the wicked will perish. So many find this an unpalatable truth that it becomes psychologically convenient to deny the reality of Noah, and the events of his day, and by extension deny the reality of a judgement on the world.

Judgement will not only be given to men but also to the angels or spirit beings. Jesus declared that "the eternal fire (was) prepared for the devil and his angels?" (Mtt. 25:41), so hell was not designed originally for mankind. The devil has a band of angels who, like him, fell by opposing God at the time of the Fall. They await judgement, but there is a small band of fallen angels who are so wicked that God will never allow them to work their evil again on the Earth. They are kept 'in eternal chains in the nether gloom until the judgement of the great day' (Jude 6). Who were they and what have they to do with Genesis 1-11?

The statement in Jude (5-7) is enigmatic; it serves to show the certainty of judgement on wicked people and does so by citing events from the early chapters of the Bible. Thus the Children of Israel, who rebelled in the wilderness, and Sodom and Gomorrah, are named alongside these fallen angels. Jude points out that they were angels, 'that did not keep their own position but left their proper dwelling' (Jude 6). They not only did that but, like Sodom and Gomorrah, 'acted immorally and indulged in unnatural lust' (v.7). Peter used the same incident in his second letter where he said that 'God did not spare the angels when they sinned, but cast them into hell (Tartarus) and committed them to pits of nether gloom to be kept until the judgement," (2 Pt. 2:4). Clearly there will be a judgement and it will include angelic beings as well as human beings.

The following interpretation is admittedly controversial but is one I make boldly believing it to be scriptually consistant. The only biblical incident to which these statements could possibly refer is found in Genesis 6:1-4. Here 'the sons of God saw that the daughters of men were fair; and they took to wife such of them as they chose' (Gen. 6:2). The term 'sons of God' refers to angels in the Scriptures in every other instance and I see no reason to doubt that it does so here. 'Their own position and proper dwelling' is to serve God in the spiritual realm but these angels lusted after human women and came to them, thereby acting immorally, and indulged in unnatural lust.' Angels, we noted before, are not allowed to or do not marry when they are in their proper position (Luke 20:34-36) but these were not satisfied with their angelic rôle.

As a result of this unholy alliance, very wicked children were born and the Earth became so corrupted that God put a 120 year limit on its course and instructed Noah to build the Ark. The Lord was sorry He made man and thus determined to do two things; a) He locked these angels away so that never again could they corrupt the Earth as they did before the Flood, and b) He decided to destroy all the wicked off the face of the Earth in a Flood and to save those who obeyed Him. We cannot grasp just how evil the world then was because today, no matter how bad our society may be and how low it sinks, there are millions of Christians with the Holy Spirit within them, working for good. Then there was just Noah ·and his family, including Lamech and Methuselah, who were still alive when the Ark was commissioned. But only eight faithful souls went into the Ark when the Flood came. Methuselah died in the year of the Flood.

God closed the door of the Ark and it was seven days before the Flood came. Legend has it that thousands tried to board the Ark once the door was shut but, whether or not this is true, the silent witness of the sealed Ark standing on the Mesopotamian plain for seven days is a witness to the reality that one day God's patience will run out. One day He will call a halt to wickedness and then judgement will come.

Here Genesis chapters 6-9 are crucial in the scheme of things. Without them this teaching of judgement and Hell loses its impact. That is yet another reason why I beleive in Adam and in the literal interpretation of Genesis 1-11, and why you are being challenged to do the same.

Chapter Nine

FAITH AND WORKS

One of the most common misconceptions about salvation and how it is gained today is that works do not matter!

Let me say right at the beginning of this short chapter that nobody is saved by works. Paul states this most forcefully in Ephesians 2:8-9, 'For by grace you have been saved through faith; and this is not your own doing, it is the gift of God — not, because of works, lest any man should boast.' *Nobody is saved by works; but equally nobody is saved without them!*

We referred several times in the last chapter to the Judgement-scene passage in Matthew 25. Here judgement was given not simply on the basis of faith but on how that faith was put into action. ' "I was hungry and you gave me food, I was thirsty and you gave me drink, I was a stranger and you welcome me, I was naked and you clothed me, I was sick and you visited me, I was in prison and you came to me," ' (Mtt. 25:35-36).

Martin Luther and the Protestant reformers over-reacted against the prevailing Roman Catholic doctrine of salvation by works. They realized — as Toplady shows in his hymn 'Rock of Ages' —
'Not the labours of my hands,
Can fulfil Thy law's demands,
Could my zeal no respite know,
Could my tears for ever flow,
All for sin could not atone,
Thou must save and Thou alone.'

Nobody can pay the debt he owes to God by zealous good works. The greatest, most humble, most active and dedicated, most wonderful worker who has ever lived, whoever he or she may be, has a righteousness like that of filthy rags in God's sight. Unless he or she has been 'washed in the blood of the Lamb', i.e. come to Jesus in faith and obedience to His wishes, they will be lost eternally. So emphatic were the Reformers on the doctrine of salvation by faith alone *(sola fide)* that Luther accused James of writing a letter of straw because of his insistence on works. The saved, for James, are those whose faith is 'active along with his works' and whose faith is 'completed by works' (Jas. 2:22). He concludes, 'You see that a man is justified by works and not by faith alone', (Jas. 2:24). (This is the only situation in the

Scriptures where the two words 'faith alone' are used together and they are used negatively!).

Can the two positions be reconciled or is James teaching a different gospel from Paul? Of course they can; James and Paul are in complete harmony.

Paul knew that there was nothing he could do to earn salvation and that he owed it all to God's grace. He also knew that, because of God's grace, certain constraints were put on him, the principle one being to preach the gospel. He told the Corinthian saints, 'For if I preach the gospel, that gives me no ground for boasting. For necessity is laid upon me. Woe to me if I do not preach the gospel,' (1 Cor. 9:16). He struggled to compete as an athelete does, 'lest after preaching to others I myself should be disqualified,' (1 Cor. 9:27). Paul believed that faith, saving faith, led a Christian into works for Christ and that if they were not done, it would mean disqualification. He and James were, as we said, in perfect harmony.

FAITH AND BELIEF

What is being confused here is the definition of the word 'faith'. Today the word 'faith' has come, in many minds, to mean no more than 'belief'. Belief is an essential ingredient of faith but it is not an interchangeable synonym. Belief alone is not the complete meaning of faith, if it were there would be no need to use two different words. James is really attacking this restricted definition of faith — it is not new, nothing ever is.

The faith which saves consists of several elements which could be summarized as 'trust and obey'; the first ingredient of which is belief. If we do not believe that Jesus is the Christ the Son of the Living God, anything else we do is null and void in Christian terms. Once we believe this astounding statement as a fact, we have to repent of our sins and past lives. It is impossible to believe in Jesus and still carry on living as we once did, without repenting, not trying to live as He would require. The belief we have leads us to confess to others that we are now followers of Christ. Any believer who will not confess Christ, that means to stand up and be counted when asked, will not be confessed by Jesus before God, (Mtt. 10:32-33). John 12:42-43 speaks of the authorities who believed in Jesus but because of the Pharisees they would not confess Him. 'They loved the praise of men more than the praise of God.'

Finally there is the necessary obedience to the wishes of Christ. The first act of which is to humble oneself in baptism and join His death, burial and resurrection (Rom. 6:3-5) and then to live steadfast, active lives of worship and service, fulfilling the Great Commission to ' "go into all the world and preach the gospel: make disciples of all nations, baptizing them in the name of the Father and of the Son and of the Holy Spirit, teaching them to observe all that I (Jesus) have commanded you," ' (Mtt. 28:19-20, Mk. 16:15).

Some seem to feel that once you leave the word 'belief' you enter the realm of 'works'. Repentance is not works, confession is not works, baptism is not works (we do not do it, we submit to it and it is done to us), worship is not works, service to the gospel is not works; they are all commands of Jesus to enable us to fulfil all righteousness; they are obediences done out of love for Him. He Himself submitted to John's baptism for this very reason (Mtt. 3:15).

This is what is meant by faith. Faith is far more than mere assent to the gospel. True, saving faith, leads to action both in respect of our own lives and in the world at large — this is the shaft of James 2:14-26.

NOAH AND ABEL — MEN OF FAITH

When illustrating his point about works, James chose to use Abraham — as he offered Isaac to God on the alter of sacrifice — and Rahab the harlot. The writer to the Hebrews also included Abraham and Rahab in his list of great people of faith in Chapter 11, but he also listed Abel and Noah, both of whom are found in Genesis 1-11.

These men are both taken as examples of faith and works, or faith and obedience, being blessed by God. Almost every person of faith has a verb of obedience to complete this faith, in Hebrews 11:

By faith Abel offered...
By faith Noah took heed and constructed...
By faith Abraham obeyed...
By faith he (Abraham) sojourned...
By faith Sarah received power to conceive ... since she considered him faithful (this may not seem like an obedience at first sight but she and Abraham must have believed the message (Gen. 18:9-14 and 21:1-2) and had sexual intercourse believing that Sarah would conceive at ninety years of age!)
By faith Abraham offered up Isaac...
By faith Isaac invoked...
By faith Jacob blessed...
By faith Joseph gave directions...
By faith Moses was hid...
By faith he (Moses) chose to share...
By faith he (Moses) left Egypt...

By faith he (Moses) kept the Passover...
By faith the people crossed the Red Sea...
By faith the walls of Jericho fell...
By faith Rahab gave friendly welcome...

The list seems endless; but one thing shines through, all these people of faith did not sit back and expect God to do it all. Their faith led them to work, often very hard work, over many years, but always out of love for God and belief in His word and promises.

Let us look at Noah, one of the true greats of faith; he, by faith, went and built an Ark 'for the saving of his household.' This was an even bigger act of faith than many realize who do not believe in the literalness of Genesis 1-11.

The world before the Flood was not a world like ours. The climate was very different, being sub-tropical all over, and the weather was vastly different too. I have discussed this elsewhere[1] but it appears that the world then was watered by a mist (Gen. 2:6). It was only after the Flood that Noah saw the rainbow. Rainbows form in small, suspended water droplets which are found in the air behind a storm. They are never found in an advancing rain cloud. Thus if you see a rainbow, the storm has passed, or that particular cloud has at least. Storm clouds and heavy rain were unknown to Noah before the Flood.

Now put yourself into Noah's position. God told him about a coming flood which would destroy the Earth. Noah did not even know about rain let alone flooding! He believed God. He did not say that there has never been a flood or, "what are you talking about God?" He preached and his contemporaries mocked. Why should they accept his word? 'Faith is the assurance of things hoped for, the conviction of things not seen," (Heb. 11:1). Noah had the assurance of salvation and the conviction that God would do as He said He would.

The question posed by the title of this chapter is "would Noah have been saved from the Flood if he had not built the Ark?" Of course not; to be saved he had to have faith, *but his faith needed to be manifest in works.* Not only did Noah have to go and do something because of his faith (just as Paul had to go and preach), he also had to do it to the specifications which God laid down.

God gave Noah detailed instructions on how to build an Ark. Nobody had ever done that before, so Noah could not have known that the ratios of 300:50:30 are the most stable for floating structures. Built to that ratio, it would be very hard to sink in the worst weather, unless it were holed.

Would Noah have been saved if he had built it to different ratios? — No.

Would Noah have been saved if he had built it of oak or ash instead of Gopher wood? — No.

Would Noah have been saved if he had not put pitch inside and out? — No.

Every lick of tar, every nail and board was a testimony to faith, in works. It was also a testimony to obedience. When I say 'works' it does not mean 'love God and do your own thing.' It is love God and do what God wants; trust and obey. It is impossible to obey unless we trust and it is impossible to trust and not obey. The two are not separate items but an intertwined truth.

Abel too showed the same loving, faithful obedience. Cain's problem was that he wanted to be acceptable to God by works — his own works — and not by faith. Abel listened to God and did as God asked. The works he did were acts of obedience. The works Cain did were his own.

It is very easy to sympathize with Cain. He brought the best fruit he had and offered it; but Abel did as God asked and not as he necessarily wanted. Abel offered a blood sacrifice, a token of the death of Christ, in obedience to God's will. By faith he looked to the final, perfect sacrifice for sins but Cain looked to his own righteousness for justification.

Would Abel's faith have saved him if he had not offered a sacrifice? — No.

Would Abel's faith have saved him if he had not offered a lamb? — No (it did Cain no good at all).

. Was Abel's sacrifice a work to gain salvation? — No, it was a loving act of obedience to the God he loved.

The point is made; our works do not save us at all, but our acts of obedience are as vital to our salvation as is our faith. As we said at the beginning — nobody is saved by works but nobody is saved without them.

Noah and Abel are crucial links in this doctrine and teaching. If they were myths they could not be held up as examples to be followed. This is yet another reason why, I believe in the literalness of Genesis 1-11.

NOTES

[1] *'Speak Through the Earthquake, Wind and Fire'*, by Graham A. Fisher, published by Countyvise Ltd., 1982, pages 49-56 and 77-78.

Chapter Ten

ADAM AND JESUS

This is the most serious chapter in the book, which is why it has been left until the last. All the other chapters show how a belief in Adam helps with other beliefs and makes sense of the Scriptures and the world in general, but this chapter deals with fundamental truth about Jesus and the salvation He gained for us. It shows how the position of those who accept Theistic Evolution, no matter how sincerely held, is theologically inconsistent. Jesus cannot be understood without a belief in Adam, the perfect edenic world and the Fall. He is known as 'the second Adam' and all believers, who doubt the existence of a literal Adam, are asked to pay very close attention to what is said below. To any atheists, who deny the existence of God and all things theological and who might be reading this book, this chapter has little to say. It is addressed to all believers; all who would call themselves Christians no matter how vaguely they understand that term.

The Bible portrays a very consistent picture about the Creation and some of these points have been touched on before. It shows a perfect world where sin and death were unknown and into which God placed man as the final pinnacle of all He made. Man was given a completely free will so that he could choose to love God as a free agent and not because God had pre-programmed him so to do.

This left the awesome possibility that man would one day use his freedom to oppose God. This he did and the Universe, including the world, fell. Death resulted as a physical punishment, and the Second Law of Thermodynamics came into force, i.e. that the Universe is now subject to decay, winding down, losing heat, and is moving from a state of order to a state of chaos. Spiritual death, a much more serious problem, also came into being and there was no way that this could be put right by any efforts on man's part. Man may climb socially and improve his physical surroundings but spiritually he was and always will be decadent and devoid of hope.

Only God could restore man to his former glory and that is through His grace as a gift. Man could not earn it or come to deserve it. To achieve this, God required a perfect sacrifice for sins and, since nobody could pay it for him, God had to send His only Son to do it. Christians believe that the man, Jesus of Nazareth, was that Son of God and that, in His death on a cross nearly 2000 years ago, He paid the price which God demanded for sin. As a result, all who believe in Him and accept His gift as He asked them to, are immediately restored to the spiritual state they once had in Adam.

GENESIS AND EVOLUTION

This is a far cry from the picture which is painted by an evolutionary 'artist'. Here the scene goes something like this; the world has evolved over thousands of millions of years. It began with gravity waves tearing a vacuum apart in a hot big bang some 15,000,000,000 years ago. Matter was created and some bits were drawn together to form galaxies. As the hot gases cooled, planets formed about 4,500,000,000 years ago and life bagan to emerge, possibly 1,000,000,000 years ago. Chemical evolution of amino-acids created the ingredients for life and, as simple structures emerged, so life began. In time these simple life-forms became more complex (the Second Law of Thermodynamics notwithstanding) and through a series of mutational changes life moved from the aquatic, to the amphibian, to the reptilian and avian, to mammalian with man at the end of a very long chain of chance. Death and survival determined the quality of the species and man has moved ever upward on a path of progress. This includes not only his physical progress but also his spiritual. Thus former religions were primitive and crude, now they are sophisticated and complex, but in his quest for truth man is moving inextricably closer to perfection. Imperfections of any sort will disappear as man masters things.

The two views cannot be reconciled. Theistic Evolutionists try, with great sincerity in most cases, to marry the orthodox scientific picture with the orthodox biblical one. Thus they re-interpret Genesis One in theories like the Day-Age theory, the Gap theory, the Two Creations theory, or simply dismiss it as a myth which teaches truth but not in a literal way. All of this produces erudite scholarship but forgets that it is Jesus and His resurrection which is the horse that pulls the theological cart. Our understanding of Creation depends on our understanding of Christ.

The biblical position is that man is the prime object of God's love and interest. He did not occur by chance or by Divinely guided chance which is a contradiction in terms, and is not the logical outcome of a belief in a God-guided Evolution. Whereas, under an Evolutionary umbrella man is no more than a superior animal who is destined to become another creature given enough time; under a Creationist umbrella he is the completed point of all Creation. Man gets lost admidst all the other creatures if the orthodox scientist is correct, but is singled out to rule and have dominion over the world if the Bible is true. The Bible asserts the distinct humanity of man, apart from nature, but Evolution places him at the animal level as part of nature.

Such divergent views prescribe different solutions to man's problems. When wrong is done, one calls it SIN and the other says that it is natural, or the product of a psychological, sociological, or enviromental imbalance.

The remedy in the first case is repentance and a change of heart; in the second it is to try to educate or psychoanalyse, the person and improve the enviroment; but rarely if ever to blame the individual and make him feel guilty. If man is only a superior animal, we must not be too surprised if he behaves like one; if he is a living soul, then we must condemn his sins and be able to expect better of him.

WHY JESUS

If God fashioned man from imperfection to perfection over millions of years, why did He need to send Jesus? If He made man perfect and then man fell, there is no need to query, "Why did my Saviour come to Earth?". A man who evolved physically and spiritually could continue his evolution, guided by God, until the perfection to which he was moving was attained. All who have gone before are merely stepping stones along his path to glory. Jesus is redundant or totally enigmatic. The fact of Jesus[1] is testimony to the falsity of such thinking.

If this is true logically what can be said about it theologically?

Jesus only makes theological sense against a biblical blackcloth. He saw Himself as the Messiah, foretold in the Old Testament Scriptures, who came to defeat Satan and lift men up. In no way did He see Himself as part of a long chain of chance, merely giving men an extra push in the right direction. His was a ministry of restoration not acceleration. What Adam lost, Christ restored. He conquered death and regarded it as His enemy and not His ally, (1 Cor. 15:26).

It is, however, in the writings of Paul that we see the strongest links between Adam and Jesus; links which no believer can ignore. He argues from Adam to Christ in 1st Corinthians and Romans. If Adam is only a myth whose story tells truths but has no literal basis, then the story of Jesus can be reduced to that of a myth which tells truth but need not be understood literally either. Indeed many modernistic, liberal scholars feel just this way about the factual aspect of our Lord's life. They deny the Virgin Birth and His miracles; they even deny the resurrection as being literally true. They accept the truth and wisdom of His teaching and the messages it brings but see the resurrection as a statement that though His spirit lives and inspires people even today, His body still lies in the tomb. Thus Christian belief in the resurrection can be likened to the hero-worship of a megastar like Elvis Presley, who, though dead, still 'lives' in the minds and hearts of his devotees. Elvis will be forgotten in a century (or sooner) but Jesus was such an extraordinary man that He never will be; so, many people find truth and enlightenment in His words but only fabricated stories about His life. This is anathema to Paul who wrote,

'If Christ has not been raised, your faith is futile and you are still in your sins . . . If Christ has not been raised, then our preaching is in vain and your faith is in vain. We are even found to be misrepresenting God, because we testified of God that he raised Christ, whom he did not raise if it is true that the dead are not raised,'
(1 Cor. 15:17 and 14-15).

The Corinthian church had suffered from men who taught falsely about the resurrection of Christ. We have seen earlier just how crucial this doctrine is to the church and to any interpretation of Scripture including Genesis 1-11. Here Paul was writing to correct their error in the strongest possible terms. He can find no greater comparison with which to contrast Jesus, than Adam.

Just weigh these words carefully and assess their importance:

'For as by a man came death, by a man has come also the resurrection of the dead. For as in Adam all die, so also in Christ shall all be made alive,' (1 Cor. 15:21-22 emphasis mine).

Further down that passage Paul gives teaching about the sort of resurrected body Christians can expect:

'Thus it is written, 'The first man Adam became a living being'; the last Adam became a life-giving spirit. But it is not the spiritual which is first but the physical, and then the spiritual. The first man was from the earth, a man of dust; the second man is from heaven. As was the man of dust, so are those who are of the dust; and as is the man of heaven, so are those who are of heaven. Just as we have borne the image of the man of dust, we shall also bear the image of the man of heaven,' (1 Cor. 15:45-49).

It is impossible to dodge the conclusion that, as far as the Scriptures are concerned, death came into the world 'by a man'. It was not present before Adam sinned. Likewise the victory over death came by a man; it was not present before Jesus was raised. It was not a policy of the survival of the fittest which was based on a 'dog-eat-dog' situation by which Adam was formed. Similarly it needed a man to effect salvation; it is not a natural process. It took a man to bring death and another man to restore life. Death did not occur because of the sins of many men for if it did, then salvation too could come via many men. Christianity claims exclusively that Jesus and Jesus alone can give life and that Adam, a single, literal man, brought death. To deny that Adam existed is effectively to deny the reality of Christ's work on the cross.

Now we can see why it is the death, burial and resurrection of Jesus which pulls the theological cart and not our views on Creation. If we determine that Jesus died and rose again, we must accept that what He did was to put right what Adam began and others have willingly followed. If we deny the existence of Adam, it is a small step to denying the work of Jesus (though most Theistic Evolutionists admittedly do not take that final logical step). Evolution then is a doctrine of atheism and is a teaching of anti-Christ! It is as serious as this!

As if to underline the literalness of Adam, Paul argues from his physical reality to the spiritual reality of Jesus. Adam is the archetypal physical man just as Jesus is the archetypal spiritual man, and the second Corinthians' passage quoted above, amply illustrates this point. The only way to escape what Paul is saying is to deny the inspiration of the Scriptures or to declare that he was a man of his day and naturally accepted a literal Adam.

Either way this is to say that Paul was merely a human being whose word has no more validity than mine. But it is impossible to keep the teaching about Jesus and jettison the teaching about Adam. If the inspiration of Scripture is denied, each person can decide for himself what he accepts, he can rewrite Scripture to suit himself but, if he does, he must not then claim to be a Christian. He can be any other 'ian' he chooses but not a Christian! For if Paul was merely 'a man of his day' in his thinking about Adam, he was also 'a man of his day' in his thinking about Christ. He can be no more correct in one, necessarily, than in the other.

If we can re-interpret one Adam to fit the latest scientific dogmas, we can certainly re-interpret Jesus also to fit the latest scientific understanding of things. This simply replaces Scripture with science and changes one authority for another. The main snag with this line of action is that scientists are forever altering what they believe so that yesterday's scientific heresy is today's orthodoxy and tomorrow's 'fairy tale'. The great god — Science — is notoriously unstable and most unreliable.[2]

The Corinthian passage would be quite enough to argue from Christ to Adam but there is an even stronger passage in Romans 5. It makes precisely the same points as above:

> 'Therefore as sin came into the world through one man and death through sin, and so death spread to all men because all men sinned... Yet death reigned from Adam to Moses, even over those whose sins were not like the transgression of Adam, who was a type of the one who was to come.
>
> 'But the free gift is not like the trespass. For if many died through one man's trespass, much more have the grace of God and the free gift in the grace of that one man Jesus Christ abounded for many. And the free gift is not like the effect of that one man's sin. For judgement following one trespass brought condemnation, but the free gift, following many trespasses brings justification. If, because of one man's trespass, death reigned through that one man, much more will those who receive the abundance of grace and the free gift of righteousness reign in life through the one man Jesus Christ.
>
> 'Then as one man's trespass led to condemnation for all men, so one man's act of righteousness leads to acquittal and life for all men. For as by one man's disobedience many were made sinners so by one man's obedience many will be made righteous,' (Rom. 5:12-19).

Paul was talking about the law of Moses as opposed to the freedom of Christ and this passage is a clear argument from one to the other. He was showing how sin came in with Adam and was not nullified by the Law. Indeed it was given greater definition by the Law and only relieved by Jesus, who both kept and fulfilled it.

This passage is like watching a tennis match from the sidelines — your head moves from left to right and back again as the ball is hit over the net. Adam is on one side and Jesus on the other, and the game swings to and fro. Every move by Adam is countered by Christ whose 'play' is far superior.

Paul was speaking of the spiritual reality of Christ's great work on the Cross. He was contrasting Christ's life of obedience in all matters of the Law — in full obedience — and Adam's failure to keep one simple law. He is writing about the eternal punishment for sin because of Adam and the great free gift of God's grace in Christ. To follow one man only brought death, spiritual and physical; to follow the other brings life.

Referring to Adam, and Christ, Paul uses the term 'one man' as if to score the point. It was ONE MAN'S fault for sin and condemnation: it is ONE MAN'S righteousness which brings justification. Ten times Paul contrasts ONE MAN with the other. Adam is no figment of primitive man's imagination. He was the one who fell and thereby caused the misery of the world. Jesus is the one who rose and brought release; it does not come by lifting one's own bootstraps (Evolution), it comes by God's grace as a gift — unearned.

Theistic Evolution is essentially a doctrine of salvation by works, with 'man as the master of things'. This is not the gospel preached by Paul, James or Jesus nor should it be by anybody who purports to be Christian. Salvation is by faith as a gift of God, unearned and unearnable, unmerited and undeserved. If Adam was unreal, this argument is unreal too. The gospel of grace is bastardized and an illegitimate changeling takes its place.

CONCLUSION

As intimated at the beginning of this chapter, the issues discussed here are very searching for the Christian. There are many believers in Christ who sincerely doubt the existence of Adam because of the pressures of science and the media today. Equally there are many who have never given these issues any serious thought at all. They are as vague about Evolution as they are about Creation, having no opinion at all because they have never studied it. They feel that Evolution must be correct because very clever men say it is.

There are many books written by equally learned men which show, scientifically, how questionable Evolution is (see Bibliography). This has been written to explore questions where a belief in Adam and Genesis 1-11, which is all too frequently labelled as myth, can help. I am convinced that far too many of today's social, political and religious problems have been created by sloppy thinking in this area.

In this chapter, conclusions have been pushed as far as possible. We noted that Evolution, even so-called Theistic (God-controlled) Evolution, is a denial of Christ and therefore, in the last analysis, must be anti-Christ. It is a doctrine of atheism not theism, and of salvation by works and not by grace. The very Christ-ness of Jesus is undermined and devalued if we do not accept Adam, since the doctrine of Jesus as the second Adam is an absolutely crucial one in New Testament thinking. If Adam was a myth, there is every reason to suppose that Jesus was too. This is serious and all believers must sit down and decide their position on this, not by learned studies in Genesis but by simple studies about Jesus. The Bible is about Jesus. The world, nay, the Universe is about Jesus. Once we get our thinking about Jesus straight then we are able to put Adam, Noah and the Flood, Cain and Abel and even Methuselah into perspective. It may not be easy but it has to be done.

For me it is never just an option on how I interpret Genesis 1-11 and that it does no matter ultimately what I conclude. I believe that serious questions about our Saviour are at stake. That is where I start, and *I conclude* that no thinking Christian can reject a literal Adam, since an understanding of Adam and the Fall is basic to an understanding of the Cross and salvation.

That is why 'I believe in Adam', and why the challenging question "Why believe in Adam?" has been posed.

NOTES

[1] Accepting the Christian belief that Jesus is the Son of God and Saviour of the World.

[2] See *'Beyond Science'*, Denis Alexander, pub. Lion Publishing, 1972.

BIBLIOGRAPHY

Alexander, Denis, *Beyond Science*, Lion Publishing, 1972.
Andrews, Prof. E.H., *Christ and the Cosmos*, Evangelical Press, 1986.
Andrews, Prof. E.H., *God, Science and Evolution*, Evangelical Press, 1980.
Andrews, Prof. E.H., *From Nothing to Nature*, Evangelical Press, 1978.
Baker, Sylvia, *Bone of Contention*, Evangelical Press, 1976, 2nd Ed. Rev. 1986.
Bowden, Malcolm, *Ape Men, Factor Fallacy?*, Sovereign Publications, 1977, Rev. 1981.
Bowden, Malcolm, *The Rise of the Evolution Fraud*, Sovereign Publications, 1982.
Darwin, Charles, *The Origin of Species*, 1859.
Denton, Michael, *Evolution: A Theory in Crisis*, Burnett Books, 1985.
Fisher, Graham A., *Speak Through the Earthquake, Wind and Fire*, Countyvise, 1982.
Hebblethwaite, Brian, *Evil, Suffering and Religion*, Sheldon Press, 1976.
Hick, John, *Death and Eternal Life*, Macmillan, 1976, Rev. 1985.
Hick, John, ed., *The Existence of God*, Macmillan, 1964.
Lewis, C.S., *The Problem of Pain*, Geoffrey Bles 1940, Fontana, 1957.
Midgley, Mary, *Evolution as a Religion*, Methuen, 1985.
Morison, Frank, *Who Moved the Stone?*, Faber, 1930.
Morris, Henry M., *Scientific Creationism*, Creation Life Publishers, San Diego, 1974.
Patten, Donald W., *The Biblical Flood and the Ice Epoch*, Pacific Meridan Publishing Co., Seattle, 1966.
Patten, Donald W., Ed., *A Symposium on Creation* (6 vols.), Pacific Meridan Publishing Co., Seattle, Vol.I, 1968.
Rehwinkel, Alfred M., *The Flood*, Concordia Publishing House, Saint Louis, Missouri, 1951.
Setterfield, Barry, *The Velocity of Light and The Age of the Universe*, Creation Science Association (Inc.), G.P.O. Box 2035, Adelaide, S.A., 5001, Australia, 1983.
Twain, Mark, *The Mysterious Stranger*, 1916, original publishers — Harper and Brothers.
Warren, Robert Penn, *All the King's Men*, Eyre & Spottiswoode, 1948.
Whitcomb, John C. and Morris, Henry M., *The Genesis Flood*, Baker Book House, Grand Rapids, Michigan, 1961.
White, A.J. Monty, *What About Origins*, Dunestone Printers Ltd., 1978.
Wysong, R.L., *The Creation/Evolution Controversy*, Inquiry Press, Michigan, 1976.

ALSO THROUGH EYE-OPENER PUBLICATIONS
Graham A. Fisher's first book,
Speak Through The Earthquake Wind and Fire,
Countyvise (1982), ISBN 0 907768 30 X,
soft back, 156pp, illustrated, A5 format, £3.95.

Creationists who believe in a young Earth must accept that the Earth has been fashioned geologically very swiftly by a series of violent catastrophes, the greatest of which was the Flood. These catastrophes must have occurred in the lifetimes of ancient men who recorded them as miracles, as God's vengeance or as the activities of their gods. There is an ever-increasing number of people who believe that many of these dramatic catastrophic events are recorded in the biblical texts and were used providentially or miraculously by God.

Speak Through The Earthquake Wind and Fire begins by explaining the current ideas about such events and then proceeds to examine many biblical stories and passages on the assumption that these ideas are correct. Special studies include the Flood, the Exodus, Joshua's long day, the problem of Judges, Elijah, Uzziah, the book of Jonah, apocalyptical New Testament writings, imagery of Satan, etc. and present the Christian with a fascinating new tool through which to study the Bible.

(Order through Eye-Opener Publications to whom cheques etc. are payable. Foreign orders in Sterling please. Add 50p p&p for each book up to 3. Four or more copies postage free.)